· Bartholomew ·

WALK KENT

by Richard Hallewell

Bartholomew

An Imprint of HarperCollins*Publishers*

A Bartholomew Walk Guide
Published by Bartholomew
HarperCollins*Publishers*
77-85 Fulham Palace Road
London W6 8JB

First published 1994
© Bartholomew 1994

Design by Bob Vickers

Printed in Hong Kong

ISBN 0 7028 2623 5
94/1/15

CONTENTS

LOCATION MAP

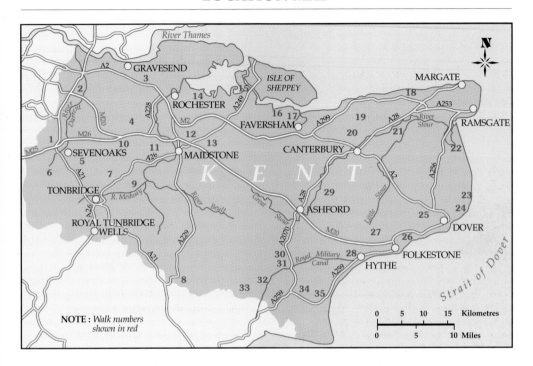

KEY TO ROUTE MAPS

Motorway		Walk Route	✆	Telephone
Major Road		Alternative Route	†	Church or Chapel
Minor Road		Other Footpath	⊼	Picnic Site
Track		Route Description	P	Parking
Railway/Station	Ⓐ	Point of Interest	WC	Public Toilet
Built up area/Building	—100—	Contour (metres)	PO	Post Office
Woodland		Stream	PH	Public House
Orchard		River	i	Tourist Information Centre
Mud and Sand		Coastline/Beach		

INTRODUCTION

(Figures in italics refer to particular routes)

Kent's common appellation, 'The Garden of England', has become something of a cliché; and a potentially misleading one at that. This is a working county, populous and busy, with its agricultural heartland dotted with thriving towns, and the industrial outskirts of London edging in from the north-west. Yet within this network of modern development – roads, railways and towns – lie the features which define the true spirit of the place: hedge-lined lanes, oast-houses, red-brick and half-timbered buildings, squat-towered Norman churches, or the wide panoramas of quilted farmland from the wooded North Downs. Such places remain to be discovered by visitors to the county, and what better way to do so than on foot?

Kent occupies a peninsula, with the River Thames and its estuary to the north and the English Channel to the east and south-east. Along its inland borders, the county marches with London to the north-west, Surrey to the west, and Sussex to the south-west. In extent, it is approximately 60 miles (100 km) from the Surrey border to the most easterly point of the Isle of Thanet; around 40 miles (65 km) from the northern edge of the Hoo Peninsula, on the Thames Estuary, to Dungeness. Within this area there is great variety of landscape. The northern coast is characterised by mud – acres of it. Flat fields are bounded by dykes and criss-crossed by meandering drainage ditches and creeks. Flocks of sea birds and wildfowl gather on the mudflats between the low islands of the Medway Estuary *(14,15)* or by the narrow channel of the Swale *(15,16,17)*. This is a flat, waterlogged land, prone to biting winds and redolent of some of the foggier passages from the works of Dickens (Rochester is the centre for the cult); but there are plenty of cosy, creekside inns, and on a clear, bright day this coast provides some of the finest walking in the county. Bird-watchers will find it a particularly rewarding area, while those with an interest in boats should keep their eyes peeled for remaining examples of the mighty Thames sailing barges.

Mud gives way to rock around the exposed coast of the Isle of Thanet, before returning in force in Pegwell Bay and along the dune-lined coast east of Sandwich *(22)*. From Kingsdown to Folkestone it is replaced by the great chalk cliffs: the striking conclusion of the long ridge of the North Downs *(23,24,26)*. These provide the most dramatic of the county's walks, with grassy downland running up to the edge of the undulating cliff tops, and magnificent views across the Channel, busy with sea traffic, to the Continent beyond.

West of Hythe *(28)* the coast undergoes a further transformation, with the cliffs turning inland and sinking into soft low hills, while the coastline swings south-west to follow the line of the great dyke around Romney, Denge and Walland Marshes. This is a strange part of the country, with an atmosphere all of its own. The east coast of this low, deltaic peninsula is lined by low-key resorts and holiday homes behind the long, slowly curving beach; ending at the twin lighthouses and mighty power station on the odd, lunar landscape of Dungeness. Inland, the flat, fertile farmland is scored by a labyrinth of winding drainage ditches, and crossed by narrow roads – inexplicably jinking to avoid long-lost obstacles – linking the tiny marsh villages with their squat, weathered churches *(33,34)*. A bleak, forlorn country in many ways, but with its own peculiar beauty. The walks here are prone to an abundance of stiles and navigational difficulties, but they offer a chance to enjoy the peculiar charm of the place.

One final thing should be said about the Kent coast: it moves. All coastlines are in a state of slow transformation, with erosion here leading to silting there, but few British coasts have changed as dramatically as Kent's in so short a period. In Roman times, Thanet was as much an island as Sheppey, and the Wantsum Channel *(18)* was an important shipping route, but land reclamation and the build-up of silt from the River Stour slowly closed the channel to navigation. Isle of Oxney *(32,33)* was likewise a true island until comparatively recent times, with the estuary of the River Rother curving to the north of it. The reclamation of the marshes from the Roman period onward ensured that, by the sixteenth century, the Isle was surrounded by fields where once there had been shallow, muddy inlets. By dint of similar processes, three of the four original Cinque Ports in Kent (pronounced 'sink': the most important of the medieval ports, which were required to supply English kings with a navy in return for tax benefits, etc.) have virtually lost contact with the sea. New Romney, where ships could once berth alongside the church, was scuppered by a freak storm which shifted the mouth of the River Rother from Romney to Rye, and is now a mile (1.5 km) behind the beach; Hythe harbour likewise vanished completely; while Sandwich is now some four miles (6.5 km) up the River Stour, and can be reached only by small boats. Only Dover – given some protection from the sands by its flanking cliffs – retains its importance.

Inland, the land changes more slowly, and the Romans would still recognise the county's major geological feature: the eastern end of the chain of the North Downs. Entering the county From Surrey, the ridge passes to the north of Sevenoaks and Maidstone before turning south, between Canterbury and Ashford, to conclude dramatically at the White Cliffs of Dover. On the northern side of the range the slopes are shallow; on the southern edge the hills break off in an abrupt escarpment, providing splendid views southwards across the Weald and the lower hills of the Greensand Ridge. The Downs provide the most spacious of the inland walks: long stretches of either open downland (27,29) or dense woodland (4,12,13); the hills occasionally crossed by narrow, high-sided roads, etched into the soft stone by centuries of rainfall and generations of travellers, but otherwise free of obstacles. Elsewhere, the interior is largely comprised of rolling farmland, crisscrossed by small roads and dotted with hamlets, villages and towns, ancient and modern, and areas of parkland and woodland. Of the parks, the most extensive is the deer park at Knole, Sevenoaks (5), with its cropped grassland and noble trees. Of the broad-leaved woods, the most extensive is Mereworth Woods (10), which contains large areas of sweet chestnut coppicing (coppicing – which can also be seen at Farningham (2) and Trosley (4) – involves cutting the tree back to the ground periodically so that it produces long, straight, poles,

suitable for fencing and other uses). Elsewhere there are areas of managed, mature woodland (20), and also of commercial conifer plantations (7, 19,30).

The proximity of the Continent has ensured that the history of the county has been one of invasions and defences. The landscape is littered with reminders of attacks and of the fear of attacks. It is not possible to surmise who was the first such invader, but the first foreign landing on record is that of Julius Ceasar in 55BC, somewhere near the invisible boundary between Deal and Walmer. In the centuries which followed their full invasion, the Romans built a number of places of strength along the coast: the forts at Reculver (18) and Richborough (north of Sandwich) at either end of the important Wantsum Channel, another at Dover (24) (the lighthouse is still standing within the castle), and a fourth, Stutfall Castle (28), by a long-vanished harbour to the west of modern Hythe. After the Romans had departed, the remaining Romano-Celts were invaded by the Germanic peoples of northern Europe (the Anglo-Saxon Chronicle states that the first arrivals had been invited by King Vortigern to aid him in his struggles with his neighbours), with the first group, under Hengist and Horsa, landing at Pegwell Bay in 449. The site is now marked by a viking ship; brought across the Channel by a Danish crew in 1949 to commemorate the 1500th anniversary of the event. Pegwell Bay also saw an invasion of another kind in 597, when St Augustine arrived with his monks to bring Christianity to the benighted English.

By the middle of the 8th century the pagan Danes had begun to harry the coast, and in 1066 the Normans landed at Hastings (next door, in Sussex). The Normans encouraged the growth of the Cinque Ports, and maintained defences at Dover. The existing Dover Castle was started by Henry Il, while the string of three castles at Sandown, Deal and Walmer was built by Henry VIII at the time when he had broken with the church of Rome and had been excommunicated as a result. In the late 18th/early 19th century, with the rise of revolutionary and Napoleonic France, the fear of invasion waxed again. The town of Deal grew wealthy as a result of the large numbers of naval ships which lay in the Downs (the area of the Channel off the coast at this point) waiting for a favourable wind to see them up the Thames, while the income of many small-ship owners – particularly on the quiet coast of Romney Marsh – was augmented by the practice of smuggling through the continental blockade. There are, in addition, more tangible memorials to the Napoleonic threat. Along the coast, from Suffolk to the Solent, 103 cylindrical, three-storey towers were built, each armed with a swivel gun and two howitzers, to repel invaders. A number of these 'Martello towers' (named after a similar structure in Corsica which had successfully resisted a British attack) remain along the Kent coast. The one at Dymchurch, by Romney Marsh, is open to the public; another can be seen by the Folkestone Warren *(26)*. Additional defence of the Marsh area was provided by the Royal Military Canal *(28,31)*, which runs for around 30 miles (48 km) along the inland edge of the flats. The effectiveness of these defensive structures was, thankfully, never put to the test; the time and energy expended on their construction, however, speak volumes for the will to resist. 20th-century fears are represented by the concrete pill-boxes to be seen by the canal and on the Folkestone Downs *(27)*, and the various monuments and museums dedicated to the RAF and the Battle of Britain. Dover Castle fulfilled its final military role as the HQ for Operation Dynamo – the evacuation from Dunkirk .

Inland, the landmarks have a different quality, and speak less of invasion than of consolidation and continuity. The great Norman cathedrals at Canterbury and Rochester, and a mass of smaller churches and chapels; the country houses at Knole *(5)*, Penshurst (south-west of Tonbridge) and Sissinghurst (near Cranbrook; famous for its gardens); and the multitude of smaller houses, farmhouses and farm buildings – notably the oasthouses (built for drying hops, and a distinctive element of the Kent landscape), with their steep conical roofs.

The most obvious literary connection with the county is Chaucer's *Canterbury Tales,* the great early work of English literature, which uses as its background a group of pilgrims journeying from London to Canterbury to visit the shrine of Thomas á Becket. Becket was murdered in Canterbury Cathedral in 1170, and, following Henry II's barefoot pilgrimage to the site two years later, his shrine attracted a vast number of pilgrims. Over the next three hundred years the town and cathedral grew immensely wealthy on their custom and gifts. The plundering of the dissolution and the Civil War robbed the cathedral of many of its treasures, but both the church and the town remain places of great beauty and character. Unfortunately, this means that they are very busy during the summer: if you want to view them in any comfort it is best to visit either early in the morning or outside the tourist season.

In addition to *Canterbury Tales,* Kent has a number of other important links with English literature. Canterbury itself was the birthplace, in 1564, of the great playwright Christopher Marlowe (the actual house was destroyed during the Second World War). Marlowe was a student at the town's King's School, as were, in later years, the novelists Hugh Walpole and W. Somerset Maugham (the latter having been sent to live with an uncle at Whitstable in 1884, following the death of his parents: the town appears as 'Blackstable' in *Of Human Bondage*). The northern coastline of the county is dominated by the figure of Charles Dickens who, though he was actually born in Portsmouth, spent much of his life living in and around Rochester and Broadstairs, and has become inextricably associated with the area. Both Rochester and Broadstairs house Dickens museums, and they and their surroundings provide the originals for the backgrounds to many of the scenes in his novels (for example, Cooling – on the north coast of Rochester – which provided the inspiration for the marsh scenes in *Great Expectations,* or Cobham *(3),* with its associations with the *Pickwick Papers*). Wilkie Collins, a friend of Dickens', was another visitor to Broadstairs; working there on *A Woman in White.*

H.G. Wells was born in Bromley (now part of Greater London) in 1866, and noted with sadness the transformation of the town from a quiet country community to an arm of encroaching suburbia. He later wrote *Kipps* and *The History of Mr Polly* while staying in Folkestone. William Hazlitt was born in Maidstone, in 1778, and shares with Marlowe the distinction of providing, posthumously, the name for the theatre in his birthplace. The poet and soldier Sir Philip Sidney was born at Penshurst Place, in 1554, and attracted a literary group which included Edmund Spenser; Vita Sackville-West was born at Knole *(5)*, in 1892, and moved to Sissinghurst with her husband, Sir Harold Nicolson, in 1930. Thackeray was long associated with Tunbridge Wells; Jane Austen wrote *Pride and Prejudice* at Godmersham (between Ashford and Canterbury). William Caxton – Britain's first printer – was born in the Weald in 1422: in Tenterden, if the pub names are to be believed.

Romney Marsh, too, attracted its devotees. Wells was in New Romney *(34,35)* in 1898, recuperating from an illness, and was visited there by Henry James. James himself was a long-time resident in the beautiful little town of Rye (just over the border, in East Sussex), while Joseph Conrad and Ford Madox Ford lived and worked in and around the Marsh; Conrad writing *Lord Jim, Typhoon* and *Nostromo* while living near Postling – at the foot of the North Downs, a little to the north of Hythe *(28)*.

In short, this is a county rich in interest, with a wide range of landscape types and historical and artistic connections. The walks chosen for this book highlight the full range of Kent's variety. Footpaths, tracks and roads pass along marshland dykes, across open downland, and through woodland and farmland. There are routes included from two miles (3 km) in length to around nine miles (14.5 km); each being loosely graded as 'Easy', 'Moderate' or 'Difficult'. Nobody who is reasonably fit should be put off by the word 'difficult'; it is a relative term, and none of these routes requires anything in the nature of athletic prowess. Nor are there any particular dangers on these walks – apart from the obvious ones: cliff edges are clearly risky, and those sections of routes which follow public roads – however quiet – require extra attention on the part of the walker. Navigation, on the other hand, can be awkward: the very lack of obvious landmarks, and the large number of tracks and footpaths, can create difficulties. When planning a trip, be sure to leave time for unintended diversions.

When walking in the countryside it is necessary to follow certain simple rules of courtesy. Stick to Rights of Way (particularly when crossing cultivated farmland); leave farm gates as you find them; avoid leaving litter. Farm animals should be disturbed as little as possible, and dog owners (unless they are very sure of their animals) should keep their pets under strict control in areas with grazing animals.

These walks represent only a tiny fraction of the possible routes in the county; there are existing local guides and leaflets (available from the various tourist information centres) which outline further possibilities, while a glance at the Ordnance Survey maps will suggest still more. There are, besides, a number of long distance footpaths running through the county; most of which are touched on by one or more of the routes in this book. The best known of these is the North Downs Way, which runs 124 miles (200 km) from Farnham, in Surrey, to Dover. This is shadowed to the south by the Greensand Way, while the Saxon Shore Way follows the line of the old coast (ie, cutting inside the Isle of Thanet and the southern marshes). In addition, there are shorter walks along the Wealdway, Eden Valley Way, Stour Valley Way and others. Information on all of these can be obtained locally.

Walk 1
CHEVENING

Have done twice up + coming down! steep going up

3.5 miles (5.5 km)   Moderate

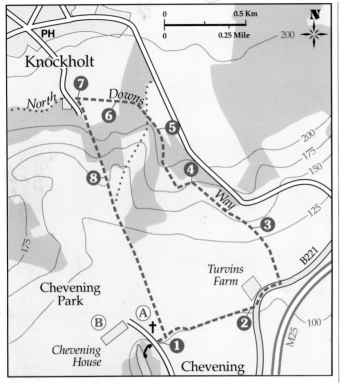

An undulating circuit on tracks and rough footpaths, following a quite complicated route through farmland and open woodland, with pleasant views over the rolling countryside to the south. Features of the route include Chevening Church and a distant view of Chevening Park. The route passes through grazing land, so dogs should be kept on a leash. To reach the start of the route, drive west from Sevenoaks on the A25 (the road for Redhill). At the village of Sundridge – about a mile (1.5 km) beyond the edge of the town – turn right onto the B221. Follow this for a mile and then turn left onto the minor road signposted for Chevening. There is no public transport link to Chevening.

Route description

❶ Go straight through the churchyard and continue beyond along a straight clear track leading to the public road.

❷ Turn left along the road. Walk past Turvins Farm and then, a short distance beyond, turn left through the hedgerow at a Right of Way sign. Continue up the right-hand side of the field beyond.

❸ At the top of the field head left for a short distance then turn right through a narrow band of trees.

Follow the line of the North Downs Way beyond, across a number of stiles and approximately following the line of trees to the right, until it reaches a stile at the bottom of a wood.

❹ Cross the stile then turn left with a long narrow field up to the right with woodland to either side of it. Cross the bottom of this field and enter the wood on the far side, then turn right, up a well-trodden path.

❺ Join the edge of the field once again and swing left along its edge. At the corner of the field a footpath cuts off to the left. Ignore this and continue until a broad lane cuts through the trees to the left.

❻ Turn sharp left at the edge of the trees, pass through a gate, then head towards a house visible on the far side of the field.

❼ Turn left just before the road, over a stile, and continue down a well-trodden footpath with a hedge to the right. Continue beyond along a narrow lane through woodland which leads to a stile at the corner of a field.

❽ Cross the stile and continue down the edge of the field. Cross a further stile and then continue along a clear track back to the church.

Points of interest

Ⓐ The oldest part of the church dates from the thirteenth century. The tower was added in the early sixteenth century, and there were later nineteenth-century additions to the building.

Ⓑ Chevening House seems to have been begun before 1630, and may be the work of Inigo Jones – although this has never been proved to everyone's satisfaction. The building was largely remodelled in the early eighteenth century. Chevening used to be the home of the Earls of Stanhope.

Walk 2
FARNINGHAM WOOD

2 miles (3 km) Easy

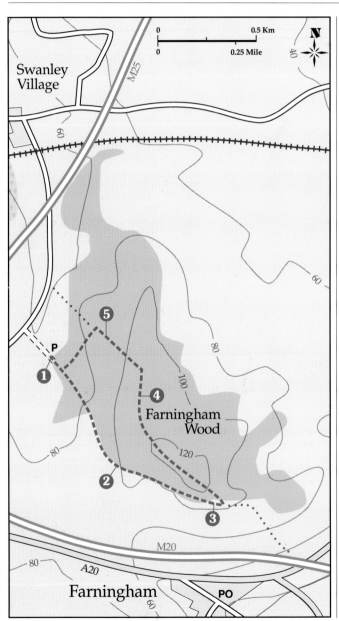

A short, pleasant, well-signposted walk on clear tracks running through a nature reserve in an area of predominantly broad-leaved woodland. The mixture of coppicing and mature trees offers a variety of habitat, making this is a good place for bird watchers. To reach the start of the route, drive south from Dartford on the A225 (the road for Sevenoaks). Five miles from the centre of town the road reaches the village of Farningham. Turn right onto the A20, then, after about a mile (1.5 km), turn right again, onto the minor road for Swanley Village. The car park is about a mile (1.5 km) along this road on the right-hand side.

Route description

❶ Leave the car park on a clear track, with a field to the right and woods to the left. Ignore the track which almost immediately cuts off to the left and continue.

❷ The field ends to the right and the track continues through woodland. Head left on the track signposted as Footpath 177.

❸ The track reaches the edge of the wood, with a view over the M20 and to the North Downs beyond. Turn left along the fence, then (almost immediately) left once again; this time following Footpath 77 back into the wood.

❹ Continue along this clear track, ignoring the rides cutting off to right and left, until, just beyond a pond, a bridleway cuts off to the left. Turn along this.

❺ At the next junction turn left once again. When this track reaches a T-junction turn right to return to the car park.

Walk 3

SHORNE WOOD COUNTRY PARK up to 8 miles (13 km)   Moderate/Difficult

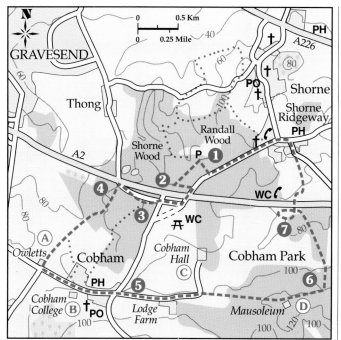

❸ At the split in the path keep right, then follow the path back on to the road for a short distance before turning left at the next arrow, back into the wood.

❹ The paths through the wood are numerous. Continue walking to the south-west until the village of Cobham is reached. Turn left along the road.

❺ At the junction at the eastern end of the village carry straight on along a clear track. When a road cuts right into Lodge Farm continue straight ahead, and when the main track turns left into Cobham Hall continue along a rougher path.

❻ Beyond the Mausoleum look for the path which cuts left back down to the road, passing to the left of Knights Place.

❼ Cross the A2 on a small bridge and continue beyond up to Shorne Ridgeway. Turn left along the public road, then left at the junction, to return to the car park.

Points of interest

Ⓐ Owletts is a red-brick Kentish farmhouse, built in 1683-4. It is open to the public on Wednesday and Thursday afternoons during the summer.

Ⓑ The church dates in part to the mid-thirteenth century. Behind it is the site of Cobham College, founded in 1362 by Sir John de Cobham. The buildings were later converted into almshouses.

Ⓒ The red-brick Cobham Hall is essentially late Elizabethan, with a central block dating from the mid-seventeenth century. The landscaping was the work of Humphrey Repton in the late eighteenth century. The Hall now houses a school.

Ⓓ The Mausoleum was built for the 3rd Earl of Darnley in 1783, but was never used.

This circuit is one of a number of possible signposted routes which begin from the Shorne Wood Country Park (a leaflet is available at the park). The route can be tricky to follow in the densely wooded sections, but it is difficult to go too far wrong. Features of this particular route include the village of Cobham and a distant view of Cobham Hall. Parts of the route follow public roads: due care should be taken on these sections. To reach the park, drive north-west from Rochester on the A226 (the Gravesend Road). A little over a mile (1.5 km) beyond the edge of the town, at Higham, turn left onto a minor road leading to Shore Ridgeway. Drive straight through this village and watch for the signs for the park to the right. PUBLIC TRANSPORT: Shorne is on the route of a regular bus service running from Gravesend.

Route description

❶ From the main car park walk south (ie, towards the A2) following the signs for the Woodland Car Park.

❷ Follow the track to the road bridge over the main road. On the far side of the road drop down to the left, then double back beneath the bridge. Follow a road running parallel to the A2. At the junction with a second road, look for the yellow arrow marking the start of a path through the woods opposite.

11

Walk 4
TROSLEY COUNTRY PARK

5 miles (8 km)   Easy

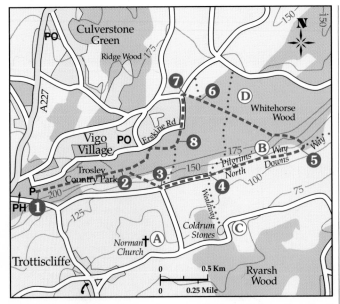

An undulating circuit, steep in places; mostly through dense woodland and coppicing, but with sections through open areas providing fine views southwards from the ridge of the North Downs. The route generally follows clear tracks and quiet public roads, with some short sections along rougher footpaths. The park and the surrounding area provide numerous alternative routes, some of which are suggested in a leaflet available from the car park. To reach the start of the route, drive five miles (8 km) east of Sevenoaks on the A25, then swing north on the A227. Once the road has crossed the M20 start watching for signs for the park to the right. There is a small fee for parking. PUBLIC TRANSPORT: Vigo Village is on a regular bus route between Gravesend and Borough Green.

Route description

❶ Leave the Country Park car park and walk along the track signposted as the North Downs Way – note the fine views to the south.

❷ There are a number of posts beside the track. Carry straight on along the main track until the third of these is reached (marked with the number 6), then turn right down a flight of wooden steps. After a short distance a path cuts off to the left. Ignore this and carry on down the hill.

❸ At the foot of the hill the path reaches a gate at the edge of park. Go through this and turn right. Almost immediately there is another gate. Pass through this and turn left along the road beyond (Pilgrims' Way).

❹ At the end of the road there is a junction, and the Wealdway cuts off to the right. Carry straight on.

❺ At the next junction the North Downs Way carries straight on. For this route, cut left over a stile and follow the path beyond, climbing through the dense woodland. When the Wealdway crosses the route, carry straight on.

❻ Join a tarmac track running across the way and turn right. After a short distance a path cuts right, onto a playing field. For this route continue on the main track, swinging round to the left.

❼ Cross a stile at the end of the track to join the public road at a junction. Turn left down a Public Byway with houses to the right. Ignore Erskine Road cutting off to the right and carry straight on until the road becomes a rough track.

❽ Continue into the trees. After a short distance there is a stile by a gate to the right. Cross this and continue along a clear track. Almost immediately there is a sign indicating a turn to the left. Follow this, and walk down through the woods to rejoin the original track. Turn right to return to the car park.

Points of interest

Ⓐ A diversion of a little under a mile (1.5 km) down the road opposite leads to the Norman church of St. Peter and St. Paul. It is built on the foundations of an earlier Saxon church.

Ⓑ Pilgrims' Way: see Walk 12.

Ⓒ A diversion of a little under half a mile (1 km) down the path to the right at this point leads to the Coldrum Stones: the remains of a neolithic long barrow.

Ⓓ Whitehorse Wood is comprised of mixed broad-leaved trees, including large areas of chestnut coppicing.

Walk 5
KNOLE PARK

7 miles (11 km)   Moderate

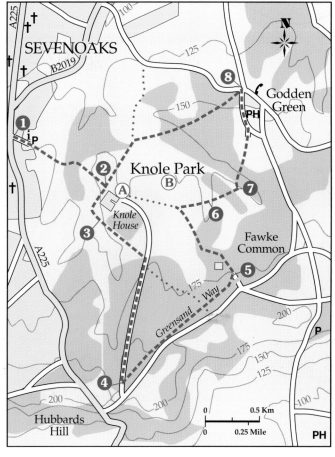

A circuit on clear tracks and footpaths through an area of undulating parkland heavily populated by fallow deer. Features of the route include Knole House and the little village of Godden Green. The walk starts from the centre of Sevenoaks; there are extensive parking facilities near the town centre. PUBLIC TRANSPORT: There are numerous rail and bus services linking Sevenoaks to London and the various Kent towns.

Route description

1 Turn off the main street of Sevenoaks following the signs for the Tourist Information Centre. Cross the car park beyond to join a footpath which leads down to a gate leading into Knole Park. Follow the rough path beyond: across a grassy swale and onto a low hill from which Knole House is visible.

2 Turn right along the face of the house, and continue until the end of the walled garden. Turn left at the corner and continue beside the wall.

3 When the wall ends carry straight on, through open parkland, until the track joins a metalled road. Turn right along this and follow it until it nears the road at the southern end of the park.

4 Turn onto the major track joining from the left and continue along it until it ends at a T-junction. Turn left.

5 Follow this track past a house, then on up the slope beyond (NB, be careful while crossing the golf course at this point). When the track approaches its highest point, look out for a grassy path doubling back to the right. Turn right onto this and follow it across a small valley.

6 After climbing the far side of the valley the path crosses another grass track and then disappears. Look for a further rough path which starts a little beyond this point; gradually becoming clearer as it leads down to the left of a stand of conifers, and then on to join a clear track beyond.

7 Swing left past the houses and continue until the track reaches a T-junction. Turn left and continue until a further T-junction is reached.

8 At this point a short detour to the right leads into the village of Godden Green. Alternatively, turn left and follow the clear track back to Knole.

Points of interest

A Knole House was begun in 1456 and was the property of successive Archbishops of Canterbury until 1532, when it was commandeered by Henry VIII. Elizabeth I passed it on to Thomas Sackville, first Earl of Dorset, who extended and improved the building. (Open to the public) .

B Knole Park comprises 1000 acres of rolling parkland and woodland. A feature of the park is the large numbers of fallow deer.

Walk 6
IDE HILL

5 miles (8 km)   Moderate

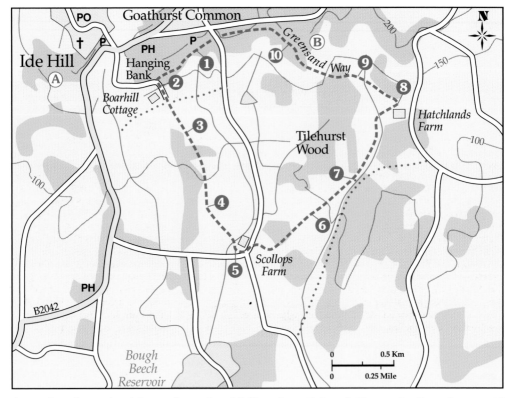

A complicated route, involving much crossing of fields and negotiating of stiles, passing through an area of mixed farmland and woodland. It is quite easy to miss the way (so some care has to be taken with the navigation), but it is pleasant walking, and there are good views south from the ridge of the Greensand Hills. To reach the start of the route, drive west from Sevenoaks on the A25 (the road for Redhill). When the road reaches Bessels Green (on the edge of the town) turn left onto the B2042. After a little under three miles (5 km) the road reaches the village of Goathurst Common. Turn left in the village on a minor road which quickly reaches a crossroads. The car park is on the far side of the junction. PUBLIC TRANSPORT: There is a daily bus service to Ide Hill – half a mile (1 km) to the west – from Sevenoaks.

Route description

❶ Cross the car park and leave it along the signposted bridleway. The paths through the woods are confusing: just angle down the face of the hill (staying to the left when the path splits) until a tarmac road is reached. Turn left down this.

❷ Just beyond Boarhill Cottage the road ends and there is a sign for a public footpath. Continue along the right-hand field boundary beyond, crossing a footbridge at the end of the field and then heading half left across the field beyond.

❸ Beyond the highest point of the field a line of trees becomes visible ahead: head for the gap. Pass through the trees and then continue straight across the field beyond, heading for a gate leading into a further area of trees. Pass through these and then walk around the left-hand edge of the field beyond.

4 Pass through a gap to the left: there are two fields ahead, divided by a hedge. Go into the right-hand field and follow its left-hand edge. Turn right at the corner, down to a stile. Cross this (into an area of woodland), then cross a footbridge over a stream and another stile beyond.

5 Continue down to the back of Scollops Farm and then to the road beyond. Turn left along this and then, almost immediately, turn right, across a stile, and follow the right-hand edge of the field beyond uphill. Cross two stiles and then continue with the wood to the left towards a stile visible at the end of the field. Continue straight on through two further fields.

6 Cross a stile and pass through a band of trees. At the far side there is a gap to the right. Ignore that and continue straight on along the right-hand edge of the next field. Continue through another field beyond and then cross a stile to reach a three-way junction.

7 Cross a stile then turn left immediately, across the end of a track, and cross another stile beyond. Continue with a wood to the right. When the fence jinks to the left, cross a stile, and the ditch and stile beyond, then follow the right-hand edge of the field beyond up to its top right-hand corner.

8 At the top of the field turn left, along the fence (part of the Greensand Way). Pass the next stile (the fence is no longer complete) and head half left on a clear path to a gate on the far side of the field. Continue beyond this to a stile visible against a wood (house visible up to the right at this point).

9 Follow the path through the woodland, rising gradually. Cross the stile at the far end of the wood and aim for two trees on the skyline ahead. From these head a little to the left of a TV mast visible beyond. Cross a stile and continue along the right-hand edge of the field beyond.

10 Cross the stile to the right and continue through the trees beyond: the path gradually swinging right before joining a clear track running along the top of the wood. Turn left along this to return to the car park.

Points of interest

A Ide Hill has a rural atmosphere with its delightful village green and church. From behind the church, there are fine views over the Weald.

B The Greensand Way is one of Kent's numerous footpaths. It enters Kent from Surrey at Crockham Hill and follows the ridge of hills on a south-easterly curve until it joins the Saxon Shore Way at Hamstreet. The Greensand Ridge offers breathtaking views, and is different to the Downs in that the land is wooded. All along the ridge are paths exploring the woodland, although many of the wooded areas were destroyed by the hurricane that ripped across south-east England in 1987.

Walk 7
DENE PARK

2 miles (3 km)   Easy

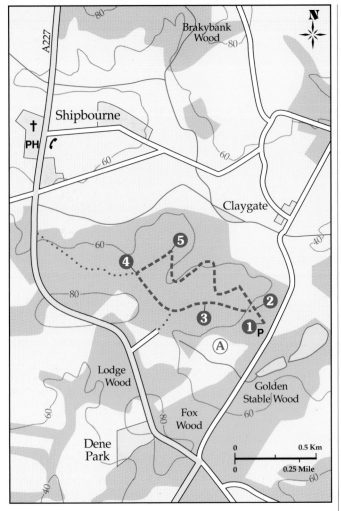

under a mile (1.5 km) along this road there is a car park to the left of the road. There is no public transport link to the walk.

Route description

❶ Leave the car park along the main track. When the track splits follow the route indicated by the 'Forest Walk' sign and black arrow.

❷ At the four-way junction turn left.

❸ Join the main track and follow it down to a T-junction. Turn right.

❹ Just before reaching a further T-junction turn right along a rougher path.

❺ At the T-junction with another small path turn right (noting the view of Shipbourne down to the left) and follow the walk arrows back to the car park.

Points of interest

Ⓐ While in the neighbourhood, it is worth visiting nearby Ightham Mote: one of the finest surviving medieval manor houses in the country. To reach it, drive north (from the car park) to the little village of Plaxtol, then turn left to reach the A227. Turn right along this, then first left on the minor road to Ivy Hatch. Turn first left once again to reach the house – a total distance of some four miles (6.5 km). Ightham Mote is a small, low, compact dwelling house (dating from the fourteenth century, but with later additions) surrounded by a moat, and was in the possession of the Selby family for nearly three centuries. The house is built round a courtyard and contains two chapels (one medieval, one Tudor) and some splendid timber work. The building is now in the care of the National Trust and is open to the public.

A pleasant, short, signposted forest walk on broad tracks and clear footpaths, passing through a mixture of conifer and broad-leaved woodland and offering occasional views of the surrounding countryside. To reach the start of the route, drive north from the centre of Tonbridge on the A227 (the road for Gravesend). A mile (1.5 km) beyond the edge of the town the road swings hard to the left and a minor road signposted for Paxtol continues straight ahead. A little

■ ■ ■ ■ ■ ■ ■   ■ ■ ■ ■ ■ ■ ■

Walk 8
HAWKHURST

3.5 miles (5.5 km)   Moderate

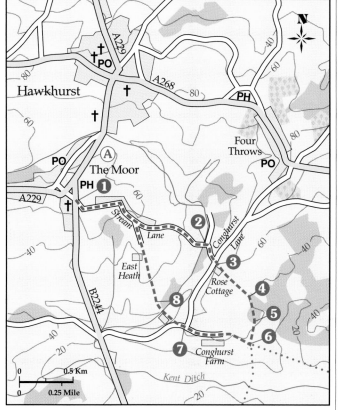

3 Turn right at the junction. Almost immediately a signposted footpath cuts off to the left, on the near side of Rose Cottage. Turn up this and pass through the gate into a field. At the end of the field pass through another gate and continue.

4 The path swings to the right around a stand of trees and then continues fairly straight before passing through a gate into a wood.

5 At the far end of the wood the path emerges at the corner of a field with a fine view over the valley below. Continue along the top of the field with a hedge to the right.

6 When the path reaches a junction with a clear track turn right. Follow this down to the public road, passing a converted oast-house on the way.

7 Turn left along the road. When this begins to swing to the left cut right onto a signposted footpath on the near side of a cottage. Start down the left-hand side of the field: the track is faint at first but quickly becomes clearer.

8 Pass through a gate at the bottom of the field then continue along the clear track, past another oast-house and down the drive beyond to return to Stream Lane.

Points of interest

A The Moor is the oldest part of Hawkhurst; a village which was once the centre of the Weald's iron industry. In the seventeenth century the iron furnaces belonged to Wiilam Penn: the founder of Pennsylvania. In the eighteenth century the village became the head-quarters of a group of ruffians called the 'Hawkhurst Gang'. They were finally captured following a pitched battle when they conducted a raid on nearby Goudhurst.

An undulating circuit through rolling farmland and woodland near the Sussex border, following quiet public roads, clear tracks and field boundaries. To reach the start of the route, pick up the A21 to the east of Royal Tunbridge Wells and follow it south for about eleven miles (18 km) to Flimwell. Turn east at this point on the A268 (the road to Rye), and follow it for three miles (5 km) to the junction in Hawkhurst. Turn right onto the A229 and park in the centre of The Moor (the adjoining village). PUBLIC TRANSPORT: There are regular bus services to Hawkhurst operating from Tunbridge Wells and Hastings.

Route description

1 From The Moor, walk eastwards along Stream Lane.

2 After crossing the stream a road joins from the left. Ignore this and continue up the hill beyond.

Walk 9
EAST PECKHAM

3 miles (5 km)   Easy

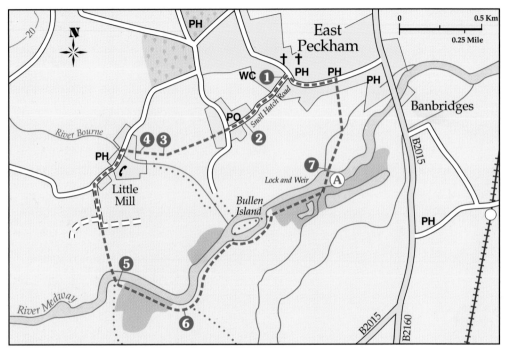

A short, gentle circuit on tracks, footpaths and public roads, running through farmland and woodland and following the bank of the leisurely River Medway. The route is clear and the going easy. A feature of the route is the river lock near the end of the walk. To reach the start of the route, drive four miles (6.5 km) north from the centre of Tonbridge on the A26 (the Maidstone Road). A little beyond Hadlow turn right onto the minor road signposted for East Peckham. PUBLIC TRANSPORT: East Peckham is served by regular bus services from Maidstone, Tonbridge and Tunbridge Wells.

Route description

1 Start from the Merry Boys public house and walk down Snoll Hatch Road.

2 Pass the old post office on the corner to the right and look for the sign for the footpath to Little Mill starting almost opposite. Cross a stile after a short distance.

3 Go through a field entrance and then continue, half left, with a fence to the left. Ignore the bridge to the left crossing the River Bourne and carry straight on.

4 Follow the river up to the public road and turn left over the bridge. When the houses end to the left turn left onto the footpath signposted for the River Medway. Ignore tracks turning off and continue straight ahead to the bridge over the river. Cross this.

5 On the far side of the bridge turn left on the path signposted for Branbridges. Ignore the broad track which swings away from the river and continue along a smaller path by the bank.

6 The path leaves the trees and continues through an open area.

Continue by the river, passing Bullen Island, going through a further band of trees, then turning left over a weir and lock gate.

7 Follow the grassy track beyond: crossing a bridge and then continuing into East Peckham. Turn left at the junction to return to the start.

Points of interest

A Sluice Weir Lock is the fifth upstream on the River Medway. The introduction of locks on the river, in the 1740s, made East Peckham a thriving port. Trading on the river ceased in 1909.

18

Walk 10
MEREWORTH

5.5 miles (9 km)   Moderate

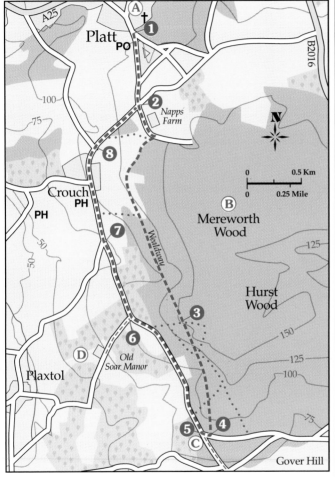

A lineal walk on public roads and clear tracks through an extensive area of mixed woodland with a possible alternative return route along quiet public roads. Great care should be taken when walking on the public roads. To reach the start of the route, drive eastward from Sevenoaks on the A25 for six miles (9.5 km) to the village of Platt. Park in the village. PUBLIC TRANSPORT: Platt can also be reached by rail (Borough Green station is one mile west of the start of the walk) or by bus (there is a regular bus service between Borough Green and Maidstone).

Route description
1 Walk southwards (ie, away from the A25) from St Mary's church in the centre of Platt. Almost immediately there is a junction. Turn right onto the road signposted for Crouch and follow it out of the village.

2 When the main road swings to the right, carry straight on along a road signposted for Napps Farm. When this road begins to swing to the left, carry straight on along a bridleway through the woods. The track, signposted for the Wealdway (WW), starts just to the right of a field entrance.

3 The first of three four-way junctions. Carry straight on at each.

4 At this point, either return to the start along the same route or turn right onto the public road. If this alternative is taken, the rest of the walk will be on public roads, and due care must be taken of traffic.

5 Turn right at junction and continue along a narrow public road.

6 A detour to the left at this junction leads to Old Soar Manor: a thirteenth-century manor house maintained by the National Trust and open to the public. This detour adds half a mile (1 km) to the walk.

7 Continue straight on at the junction into the village of Crouch. Walk straight through the village, ignoring the road cutting off to the left.

8 At the junction beyond Crouch keep right and continue along the road back to Platt.

Points of interest
A St Mary's church: built 1841-42.

B Mereworth Wood comprises one of the most extensive areas of unbroken woodland in Kent. The trees are principally broad-leaved, including large areas of coppicing.

C Turn left at this point for quarter of a mile (0.5 km) to reach Gover Hill (National Trust). There are fine views from the road across the valley of the Medway.

D Old Soar Manor is the remaining section of a fortified manor house built in the thirteenth century for the Culpeper family.

19

Walk 11
MANOR PARK

4 miles (6.5 km)   Moderate

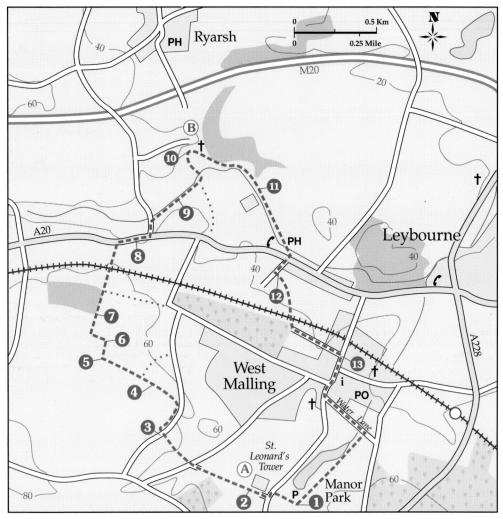

A complicated circuit of paths, tracks, public roads and field boundaries through an area of farmland and mixed woodland; some care will need to be taken with the navigation and when walking on the public roads. To reach the start of the route, drive six miles (9.5 km) west from the centre of Maidstone on the A20 (the road for Sevenoaks). After crossing the junction with the A228 take the next turn left, into West Malling. Drive straight through the village and watch for signs for the Country Park to the left of the road. There is a large car park and a small fee for parking. PUBLIC TRANSPORT: There is a railway station in West Malling, and the village is on bus routes from Maidstone, Tonbridge, Tunbridge Wells, Chatham, etc.

Route description

1 Leave the car park on the footpath leading back to the road. Cross the road and follow the track beyond, to the left of the tower.

2 Follow the track beyond the tower to a road. Cross the road and continue along the public bridleway beyond.

3 Cross the next road and go over a stile into a field. Turn right along the edge of the field. Cross a track and then continue around the edge of the next field.

4 At the corner of the field cut half right, into a stand of trees. Once through the trees head half left, following a well-trodden path along the edge of a field. At the corner of the field jink half right and then continue along the left-hand edge of the next field.

5 The track swings round to the right, still along the edge of the field, then continues for a short distance with a stand of trees to the left.

6 Turn left at the end of the trees along a broad track. At the end of the field turn right, off the track, and continue along a clear path with a hedge to the left. Carry straight on, crossing two stiles, until the path reaches an area of woodland.

7 Continue straight downhill, with the wood to the left, crossing a bridge over the railway line and dropping down to the A20. Turn right along the road.

8 Cross the road (taking care) and, after a short distance, turn left on the road for Ryarsh Village Hall. Just before this road crosses a small stream there is a sign for the path to the right. Go through the gate into a narrow meadow. When the path splits, keep to the left.

9 At the far left-hand corner of the field there is a stile. Cross this and continue along the left-hand edge of another narrow field. Cross the stile at the far end and turn left across a footbridge over a stream. Cross a further stile and continue along a clear track beyond.

10 Turn right at the end of the hedge and continue towards the church. Walk through the churchyard and pass through a gate at the far end. Turn right along the tarmac track beyond .

11 Follow this track until it passes to the left of a house. Turn right beyond this, up a tarmac track leading to the A20. Cross the road and continue up Brickfields Lane beyond. Turn left beyond the second cottage.

12 Behind the cottage the track splits. Go right, through a tunnel of bushes at first, then between two hedges. Cross the railway line and then head half left down to the end of Ryarsh Lane. Follow this to the main street.

13 Turn right into West Malling, then left into Water Lane. A little beyond Ewell Monastery turn right, into Manor Park: follow the ridge above the lake at first, then head half left to reach the car park.

Points of interest

A St Leonard's Tower was built beside a Norman church of the same name at the end of the eleventh century (making it one of the earliest pure Norman buildings still standing in Britain). There has been some dispute as to whether it was intended to be part of the church or an independent defensive structure: the latter seems more likely.

B St Martin's Church, Ryarsh, is part early Norman, but with additions dating from the fourteenth century.

Walk 12
BOXLEY

4 miles (6.5 km)   Moderate

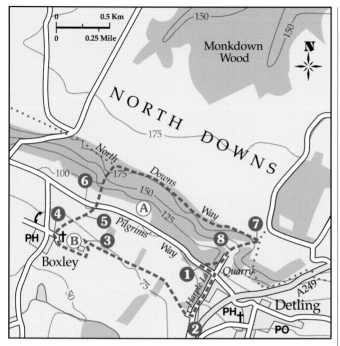

An undulating circuit, steep in places, passing through dense woodland on the ridge of the North Downs, and open farmland on the lower ground. To reach the start of the route, drive north from Maidstone on the A229. Turn left at the roundabout near the edge of the town (signposted for Boxley), then right at the next major junction, up Boxley Road. Turn right just beyond the village and park in one of the parking places a little before the road reaches its next junction – a distance of about one mile (1.5 km). PUBLIC TRANSPORT: Maidstone is well served by rail and bus services; Boxley can be reached by an infrequent bus service from Maidstone.

Route description

1 Start walking from one of the parking places on the Pilgrims' Way. Head eastwards (ie, with the ridge of the Downs to the left) until the road reaches a junction. Turn right down Harple Lane.

2 Follow this road until, just after the final house on the right-hand side, a track cuts off to the right. When this track begins to swing to the left it is crossed by a gate. Just beyond the gate there is a stile to the right. Cross this and continue along the bottom of the field beyond, with a line of hawthorns to the left.

3 A house is reached to the left of the path. Cross the fence to the left and double back for a very short distance, then cross another stile and turn right inside a field with the house to the right. Rejoin the original track and turn right along it to reach Boxley.

4 Turn right past the entrance to the church and turn right over a stile into a field. Walk up the edge of this field with a fence to the left.

5 At the top of the field cross another stile and continue along a faint path beyond. At the top of this next field cross a further stile and veer left, straight up the slope to the road. Cross the road and continue up the path beyond, climbing steeply up the face of the Downs.

6 Ignore a large track joining from the right and continue until the top of the ridge is reached. At the junction with the clear track of the North Downs Way turn right and continue through dense woodland.

7 When the track reaches a T-junction turn right. After a short distance the North Downs Way is signposted to head off to the left. Ignore this and carry straight on. When the track splits keep to the right (the other branch leads to a house).

8 The track passes the entrance to a quarry at the top of a tarmac road. Continue along this road for a short distance and then turn right onto a footpath running through the woods. Follow this back down to the Pilgrims' Way.

Points of interest

Ⓐ The name 'Pilgrims' Way' suggests a medieval origin for this ancient route linking Winchester to Canterbury and Dover. In fact, it is thought to be much older than that: a prehistoric trackway which followed the dry, elevated Downs in preference to the sticky clay of the Weald.

Ⓑ The original church was Norman, and was greatly extended in the 13th century. The tower was added in the 15th century and the exterior was renovated around 1870.

Walk 13
THURNHAM

3.5 miles (5.5 km)   Moderate

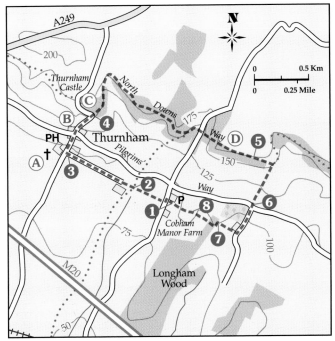

A short circuit following the ridge of the North Downs and passing through farmland at the foot of the escarpment. The route, steep in places, follows footpaths and quiet public roads. To reach the start of the route, drive east from Maidstone on the A20 road for Ashford. At Bearsted, turn left to reach Bearsted Station. To the east of this a minor road passes under the railway line and heads north for a little over a mile (1.5 km) to the village of Thurnham. Turn right at the crossroads, then right again at the next four-way junction. The car park at the riding centre at Cobham Manor Farm is a short distance down this road on the left-hand side. There is no public transport to Thurnham.

Route description

1 Walk out of the gate onto the public road and turn left for a short distance. Just before reaching a converted oast-house, turn right across a stile into a field. Walk straight on across this field.

2 Cross a further stile and continue beyond, along a tarmac area in front of a house; then go through a gate and continue, down a tarmac road leading to Thurnham.

3 When the track reaches the public road turn right, through the village of Thurnham. Cross a junction and then continue up the slope of the North Downs beyond.

4 When the road swings sharply to the left there is a signpost for the North Downs Way to the right.

Turn on to this track and follow it along the ridge: crossing a small public road at one point and then continuing beyond.

5 The track drops down to reach a T-junction at the edge of a field (fine views of the Downs ahead). At this point the North Downs Way goes left, but for this route turn right, down the slope to a public road.

6 Cross the road and then continue along a tarmac road. Watch for the Right of Way signpost in a garden fence to the right. Turn right, straight across the garden and then on along the narrow footpath beyond.

7 Cross the stile at the end of the field and head a little to the right for a short distance, across an open area, to another stile. Continue straight on beyond this through a field.

8 Cross a stile over a wooden fence and turn left along the inside of the field beyond. At the corner of the field turn right and continue beside the fence until the end of the field is reached. Cross a further stile at this point, then walk diagonally down to the car park at the riding centre, visible below.

Points of interest

A Thurnham is a pleasant, quiet village. The church is Norman with fourteenth-century additions, and was largely renovated in the nineteenth century. The Victorian cricketer Alfred Mynn is buried here.

B The road being crossed at this junction follows the line of the Pilgrims' Way (see Walk 12).

C Thurnham Castle was a motte-and-bailey keep built in the 11th or 12th century. There is little to be seen there now but tree-covered mounds.

D The North Downs Way is a 124 mile (200 km) long public footpath linking Dover and Farnham (Surrey).

Walk 14
RIVERSIDE COUNTRY PARK

5 miles (8 km) there and back   Easy

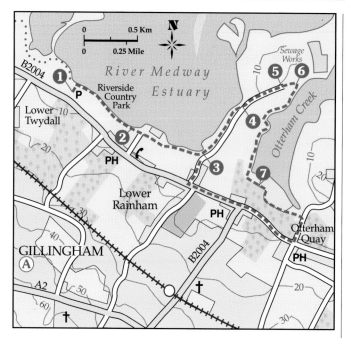

A flat, lineal, coastal route, following the edge of the mud flats which surround the broad estuary of the River Medway. The route follows clear tracks and footpaths, with a possible return by public road (this can be quite a busy road, so considerable caution should be observed). To reach the start of the route, drive north from the centre of Chatham on the A231, then turn left onto the B2004. Follow this for three miles (5 km), watching out for signs for the Riverside Country Park to the left. There is a large car park behind the dunes. PUBLIC TRANSPORT: Gillingham is served by numerous bus and rail services; there is a regular bus service from Gillingham along the B2004.

Route description

1 Walk from the car park onto the track running along the edge of the estuary. Ahead and to the left is the headland of Horrid Hill, and a shore path continues beyond that for those who wish to explore it. For this route, turn right.

2 Go past the breakers yard and continue along the shore beyond.

3 Swing to the left along the top of a dyke, with a small public road down to the right.

4 When the shore swings to the left carry on along the road.

5 Just before the entrance to the sewage works there is a stile over a fence to the right (signposted). Cross this and continue by the side of the fence.

6 Cross the footbridge over a small ditch and climb up onto the sea wall beyond. Turn right along this, with Otterham Creek down to the left.

7 At this point the path reaches the edge of an industrial complex. Either return by the same route or else skirt around the edge of the complex until it joins the public road and return that way. The first option provides the more pleasant walking and avoids the traffic.

Points of interest

A Gillingham is a relatively modern arm of the conurbation clustered around the head of the Medway Estuary. There is nothing of particular interest to be seen in it, but while in the area it is worth visiting the naval dockyard in neighbouring Chatham – three miles (5 km) west of the start of the walk – and the town centre of Rochester – two miles (3 km) beyond. Chatham began its long association with the Royal Navy when a repair yard was founded there in 1547. In the following centuries it developed into a dockyard, and attracted visitors such as Pepys, Peter the Great (a keen boatbuilder himself) and Nelson (the *Victory* was built here). The dockyard exhibits cover an 80-acre site. The attractions of Rochester include the cathedral (originally eleventh-century, but with additions up to the fourteenth), the enormous ruined keep of Rochester Castle (eleventh/twelfth centuries) and the Charles Dickens Centre.

Walk 15
CHETNEY

5.5 miles (9 km)   Easy

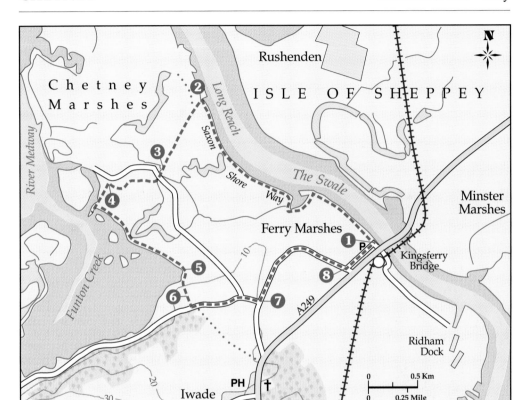

A flat low-level circuit on clear tracks and quiet public roads, following the sea wall on the southern side of the Swale, and passing along the edge of the island-dotted mud flats of the broad estuary of the River Medway. Excellent for bird-watching. To reach the start of the route, drive 12 miles (19 km) north of Maidstone on the A249. Just before crossing the Kingsferry Bridge (over the Swale) turn left, following the signs for Ridham Dock. This road swings round to pass under the bridge, but just before it does so there is a car park to the left of the road. PUBLIC TRANSPORT: There are no bus services, but the rail service to Sheerness stops at Swale Station, just to the east of Kingsferry Bridge.

Route description

❶ Climb up onto the dyke from the car park and turn left.

❷ The track swings to the left. Ignore the gate to the right and continue inland along the clear track.

❸ The track reaches a road. Cross a stile onto the road, then another on the far side to continue along the top of a dyke beyond.

❹ When the path reaches a deserted farm turn left, along the near side of the fence, and then continue down to the side of the creek beyond. Turn left along a clear path; round a small headland and on along the shore.

❺ Just before the shore of the creek swings away to the right a path breaks away and continues straight ahead, along the top of a dyke.

❻ After a short distance the path reaches a gate. Go through this then drop down to the left of the dyke. Cross a stile and then walk up the left-hand side of the fence beyond to reach the public road. Turn left along the road.

❼ Turn left at the first T-junction.

❽ Turn left at the junction to return to the car park.

25

Walk 16
CONYER

6 miles (9.5 km)   Moderate

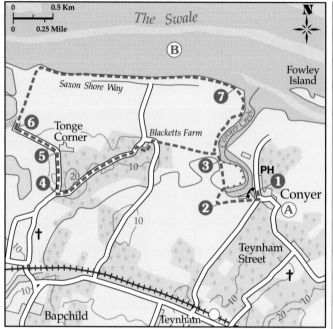

A low-level circuit on clear tracks and quiet public roads, passing along the sea wall on the south side of the Swale (the muddy channel separating the Isle of Sheppey from the mainland) and the boat-filled mud flats of Conyer Creek, and making a cast inland through open farmland and orchards. The roads on this latter section are very quiet, but care must still be taken. To reach the start of the route, drive three miles (5 km) west of Faversham on the A2 and turn into Teynham. Conyer is two miles (3 km) north of Teynham on a minor road. PUBLIC TRANSPORT: There are rail services to Teynham, while Conyer is served by a regular bus service from Sittingbourne (via Teynham).

Route description

1 Walk south down the neat terrace of houses near the end of the Conyer road (ie, walk in the direction of the main road). When the road swings hard left turn right. There are two possible paths here: take the main track, to the right, and follow it past a line of warehouses to the head of the muddy Conyer Creek.

2 Beyond the boatyard the path climbs onto a dyke. Turn right along this and follow it over a footbridge across a narrow stream. Immediately beyond this the track splits. Take the left-hand path.

3 The tracks rejoin for a short distance and then split once more. Go left again, and follow a straight track to Blacketts Farm. Turn left

before the first large barn and follow the track as it swings around behind the barn to join the entrance drive. Turn left along this.

4 At the junction of the public road turn right (signposted for Tonge Corner).

5 Pass the entrance to Tonge Corner and continue along the public road.

6 At the end of the road turn right down a clear track with a number of large lakes visible through the trees to the left. When the track reaches the dyke by the side of the Swale turn right.

7 The track swings right to follow the side of Conyer Creek back to the start of the route.

Points of interest

A Conyer is too small to be considered a village, but it has a handsome line of new houses overlooking the creek and a comfortable inn. The creek itself will be of great interest to boat lovers.

B The Swale, narrow and largely tidal, runs fifteen miles (24 km) from the Medway Estuary to the mouth of the Thames Estuary, and is typical of the type of muddy channel which would once have separated Thanet, the Isle of Grain and other ex-islands from the Kent mainland. From Roman times, such channels provided a relatively safe, sheltered route for coastal shipping moving up the Thames, and in comparatively recent times the Swale retained its trading tradition, with shoal-draft sailing barges carrying goods (principally fruit, from the north Kent orchards) to larger markets. The Dolphin Yard Sailing Barge Museum in Sittingbourne – some five miles (8 km) west of Conyer by road – includes surviving examples of these barges.

Walk 17
FAVERSHAM

5 miles (8 km)   Easy

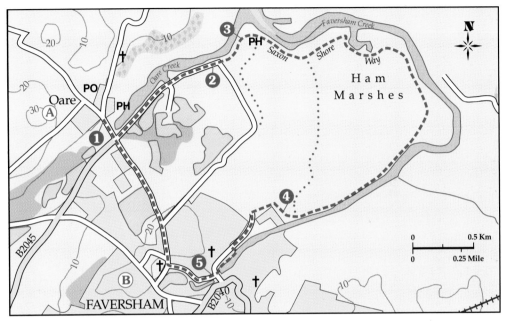

A flat, low-level circuit on public roads, tracks and footpaths, running along the shores of two of the numerous muddy creeks to be found on the edge of the Thames Estuary. The walk passes boatyards and moorings, and may provide a view of one of the surviving Thames sailing barges which still sail from these creeks. The centre of Faversham is of considerable architectural interest. To reach the start of the route; either start from Faversham itself, or drive north from the town on the minor road for Oare. PUBLIC TRANSPORT: Faversham is served by numerous bus and rail services; Oare is on a regular bus service between Maidstone and Faversham.

Route description

1 Park in Oare and walk back down the road towards Faversham. Immediately after crossing the head of the creek turn left. When the road splits keep to the left, by the side of the creek.

2 When the road swings round to the right cut left onto a signposted footpath (Saxon Shore Way) which heads back down towards the water.

3 Pass the Shipwrights Arms and the club house of the sailing club and then swing right, continuing by the waterside.

4 When the path reaches the edge of Faversham a large factory blocks the route along the shore. Turn right and skirt around the building. When the factory entrance is reached go down a footpath to the right of it, cross a footbridge over a small channel, then continue along the edge of the creek.

5 The road reaches a junction with a bridge to the left. Cross this to explore the centre of Faversham. Otherwise, cross the road ahead and carry straight on up a small industrial road. At a T-junction turn right and continue back to Oare.

Points of interest

A Oare is a small cluster of buildings on a slope above the creek. It was once a minor port, and also controlled the road leading to the ferry across to the Isle of Sheppey.

B Faversham first became important as a staging point on the Roman road linking Canterbury and Rochester at a place where the road crossed a navigable inlet of the Swale. It became a limb of the Cinque Ports in 1225. The modern town is a mixture of rather grim industrial outskirts and a splendid town centre which retains many of its old buildings.

Walk 18
WANTSUM WALK

8.5 miles (14.5 km)   Difficult

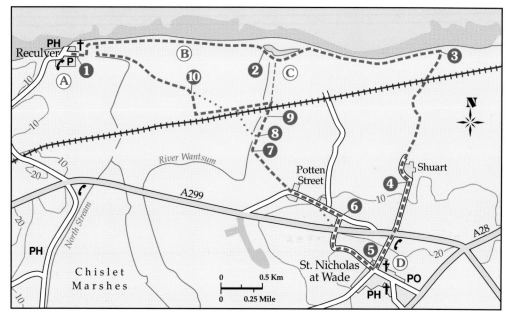

A long, flat circuit along sea walls and dykes, passing through an area which was once covered by the sea channel between the mainland and the Isle of Thanet. The first section runs behind the rocky sea shore, then the route cuts inland through marshland, scrub and farmland. To reach the start of the route, drive east from Herne Bay along minor roads, following the signs for Reculver. PUBLIC TRANSPORT: There is a railway station at Herne Bay, and a regular bus service between Herne Bay and Reculver.

Route description

1 Start from the car park at the end of the public road. Walk up to the ruins of St. Mary's Church and then continue along the sea wall beyond.

2 At the point where the sea wall swings inland for a short distance, a dyke heads off to the right. Follow this for a shortened route.

3 Turn right onto the next dyke and follow it inland, across the railway line (with due care) and on to the farm at Shuart.

4 Beyond the farm the track joins a tarmac road. Turn right along this and follow it up to the A299. There is a footbridge over the road, and beyond that a road continues into the village of St Nicholas at Wade.

5 At the junction by the church turn right and follow the road back over the A299.

6 On the far side of the bridge swing left. At the next junction ignore the road to the right and carry straight on. At the following junction carry straight on once again, across one of the drainage ditches.

7 At the split in the track keep right.

8 The track splits once more. Ignore the bridge over the ditch to the left and keep straight on.

9 Cross the railway line, climb up onto the dyke beyond, then turn left.

10 Ignore the dyke cutting off to the right and carry straight on, back down to the sea wall. Turn left to return to the start.

Points of interest

A The settlement at Reculver originated as a Roman fort and later became an important religious site. The 12th/13th-century church was demolished early in the 19th century leaving only the two western towers.

B The sea wall dates from the eighteenth century.

C The dyke cutting right marks the line of the entrance to the old Wantsum Channel: at one time an important route for shipping leading to Canterbury and Sandwich.

D The first church here was built in the 11th century. The present structure is a 14th/15th-century remodelling of an older building.

■ ■ ■ ■ ■ ■ ■   ■ ■ ■ ■ ■ ■ ■

Walk 19
CLOWES WOOD

3 miles (5 km) Easy

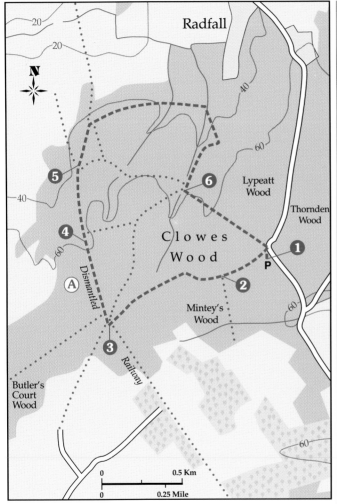

A standard forestry walk, passing through a mixture of coniferous and broad-leaved woodland. The route follows broad forestry tracks and rougher footpaths – often wet in places – and since the walk is not signposted some care has to be taken over navigation. To reach the start of the route, drive a little over two miles (3 km) north from the centre of Canterbury on the A290 (the road for Whitstable). Having reached the village of Blean, turn right onto the minor road signposted for Tyler Hill. Follow this into the village then turn left onto the road signposted

for Chestfield. A mile (1.5 km) north of Tyler Hill a road cuts off to the left. Turn up this: a short way along, by a sharp turn in the road, is the car park. PUBLIC TRANSPORT: An infrequent bus service runs between Chestfield and Tyler Hill.

Route description
1 Walk north from the car park (ie, away from Canterbury) to reach the junction of two forest tracks, just off the road. Take the left-hand track.
2 Ignore the track cutting off to the left and continue.
3 At the T-junction turn right. Ignore the track which cuts off to the left after a short distance and continue.
4 Track cuts off to the right. Ignore and continue.
5 At this point the track splits, with one track continuing straight ahead and the other swinging to the right. Stay to the right, then take the next path cutting off to the left. Continue along this track, ignoring paths cutting off to right and left.
6 When a major four-way junction is reached turn left, back to the car park.

Points of interest
A The track at this point follows the bed of the old railway line linking Canterbury and Whitstable. Canterbury had long ceased to have any importance as a harbour by the time steam technology arrived, and its citizens quickly realised that the railways offered the main hope of avoiding the decline into an economic backwater. As a result, the link was made as early as 1830; a locomotive called *Invicta* carrying passengers the six mile (9.5 km) distance in around 40 minutes. This early engine struggled with the gradients, however, and was soon withdrawn.

Walk 20
CHURCH WOOD

2.5 miles (4 km)   Easy

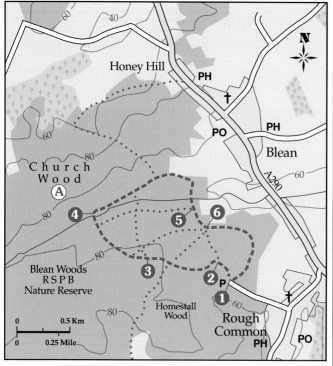

Route description

1 Follow the colour-coded sign-posts out of the car park.

2 At the first junction turn left, following the sign for the red trail, crossing one of the short cuts after a short distance and continuing.

3 Keep left at the split of the paths, again following the red signs. The track crosses two further short cuts before reaching and crossing the stream.

4 Swing right beyond the stream and continue along the clear track

5 Green trail joins from the right.

6 Brown trail joins from the right.

Points of interest

A Church Wood is part of the 7000 acres of woodland on the high ground to the west and north of Canterbury which constitutes the remnants of the old Forest of Blean – a royal forest at one time, and noted in later years as a hide-out of smugglers. Much of this remaining area has been given over to conifer plantations or sweet chestnut coppicing, but in Church Wood the natural coverage of oak, beech, birch and other broad-leaved trees has been preserved. This in turn supports a large number of species of birds, including woodpeckers, nuthatch, redstart, tree creeper, willow warbler and nightingale.

The route described is the longest of three possible routes – the others are 1.75 miles and 1 mile (3 km and 1.5 km) – laid out through the RSPB nature reserve in Blean Woods. All three routes are colour-coded and leaflets are available at the car park. The routes are clearly marked and the tracks are good. To reach the start of the route from Canterbury, follow the A290 road for Whitstable. After 1.5 miles (2.5 km) turn left into the village of Rough Common. Watch for signs for the woods to the right of the road: a long straight drive leads up to the car park. PUBLIC TRANSPORT: Rough Common is on the regular bus route between Canterbury and Faversham.

Walk 21
STODMARSH

6 miles (9.5 km) there and back   Easy

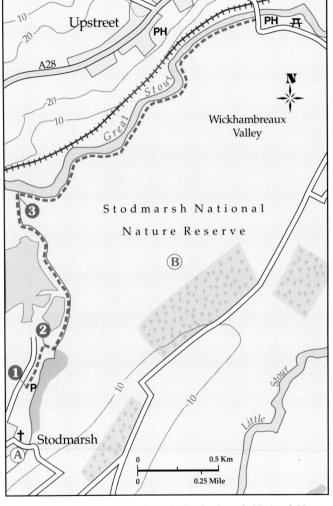

species. To reach the start of the route, drive east from the centre of Canterbury on the A257 (the road for Sandwich). Just beyond the edge of the town, turn left on the minor road for Stodmarsh (there is an alternative car park at Grove Ferry, at the eastern end of the route). PUBLIC TRANSPORT: There is a single daily post bus service from Canterbury to Stodmarsh; Upstreet (just to the north of Grove Ferry) is on the regular evening bus service between Canterbury and Ramsgate.

Route description

1 Leave the car park and follow the route indicated for the Stour Valley Walk.

2 Junction. Ignore the gate to the left and follow the main track as it swings round to the right.

3 The track joins the Great Stour. Follow this out of the Nature Reserve and on for as far as is wished. The path joins a small public road at Grove Ferry, where there is an inn.

Points of interest

A The little village of Stodmarsh is worth visiting while you are in the area. It has an inn and a restored medieval church. The name is a corruption of 'stud marsh', suggesting that the area was once known for its horse breeding.

B A large number of species are attracted by the wetlands. In the reed beds there are reed, sedge and Savi's warblers, bearded reedling, bittern and others; while the open water provides a habitat for a number of species of duck (mallard, teal, tufted, pochard, shoveler and wigeon), as well as great crested and little grebes, cormorant and a variety of waders. A more detailed listing of the local bird, insect and plant life can be found in a leaflet which can be purchased at the car park.

A flat, lineal route, running through the Stodmarsh National Nature Reserve (Nature Conservancy Council) and then on along the bank of the Great Stour. Return by the same route. The reserve covers an area of low-lying, marshy ground in which the subsidence of the local colliery has led to the creation of a series of reed banks and open lagoons. This route will be of specific interest to bird watchers (walkers are requested to stick to the paths and to keep dogs under control at all times), as the various habitats attract a wide range of waterfowl, seabirds and other

Walk 22
SANDWICH

5 miles (8 km)   Easy

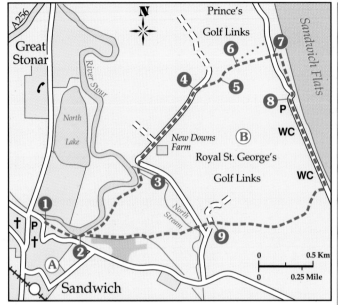

⑥ Cross the dyke onto the golf course. The route across the course to the shore is marked.

⑦ Cross the tarmac road and head towards a stile over a fence visible ahead. Turn right along the path beyond the fence.

⑧ Follow the path as it swings up to join the large car park. Just beyond the second toilet block turn right, over the fence, and follow the path beyond (marked by concrete markers) across the golf course.

⑨ After passing the 18th green cross a track and a tarmac road and continue towards the railings of a bridge visible ahead. Follow the path beyond back to Sandwich.

Points of interest

Ⓐ Sandwich, one of the most pleasant towns in Kent, has a history of fluctuating fortunes. In Roman times Richborough Castle – a mile (1.5 km) to the north – was a vital part of the coastal defences. By the eleventh century Sandwich was one of the most important ports in the south of England (it was one of the original Cinque Ports). Kent's shifting shoreline put an end to this prosperity, however, and by the mid-sixteenth century the town had lost its harbour, with the result that its population dropped to around 200. The introduction of Flemish weavers and tanners in the seventeenth century revived Sandwich's fortunes. The town is of interest today principally for its large number of surviving medieval to sixteenth-century buildings.

Ⓑ Royal St George's Golf Links: one of the premier British golf courses and occasional host to the British Open championship.

A flat, low-level circuit on clear tracks and footpaths; running by the side of the River Stour and by the dunes behind Sandwich Bay, and across the famous Royal St George's Golf Links. Sandwich is of considerable architectural interest, and is worth a visit on its own account. If driving, park in the car park on the quay by the River Stour. PUBLIC TRANSPORT: Sandwich has a railway station and is on numerous bus routes.

Route description

① Start from the car park by the quay and walk east (ie, towards the sea) by the river bank.

② Turn left across a white metal bridge over a tributary. Keep left at the junction and continue along the tarmac track to the right of the river.

③ Cross another bridge over a tributary and join a tarmac road crossing the way. Turn left along this and follow it as it swings round to the right. Walk past New Downs Farm and ignore the track which cuts off to the left a little beyond it.

④ At the next junction go right, over a stile by a white gate, and continue along a clear track to some corrugated iron sheds.

⑤ Beyond the sheds go half left and continue along the clearest track until a dyke is reached.

Walk 23
ST MARGARET'S TO KINGSDOWN

5.5 miles (9 km)   Moderate

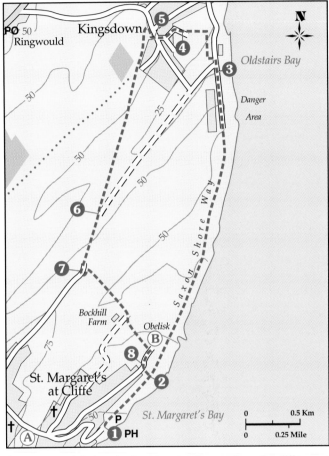

❷ Just beyond the last house the track splits. Keep to the right, and follow the path along the cliff-top until it drops down to join Undercliff Road at the southern end of Kingsdown.

❸ Follow this road for a short distance. Just before the last house to the right a yellow arrow indicates a flight of steps to the left. Climb up these, turn right at the top, and then follow the clear path beyond around the outside of a high fence.

❹ The path emerges beside a Scout Camp with a road junction ahead. Take the road which continues in the direction of the path. At the next junction turn right.

❺ At the following junction turn right once again, then first left at the sign for a Public Bridleway. Follow this straight track until it splits at the end of a row of houses. Keep left and follow a clear, straight path, over a large track and then on diagonally down the face of the slope.

❻ The path comes down to join a clear track. Continue along that.

❼ When the track reaches a junction double back to the left. After a short distance turn right and walk straight up the hill. Ignore the track to the right leading into Bockhill Farm. Near the farm there is a further arrow, pointing to the left. Follow the way indicated: over the brow of the hill and down to join a road running across the slope. Turn right, past the monument.

❽ After a short distance (before the houses) a path cuts down to the left to rejoin the original track.

Points of interest

Ⓐ The town of St Margaret's at Cliffe contains one of the finest parish churches in Kent, dating back to the third quarter of the 12th century.

Ⓑ The large obelisk on the hill to the left is a monument to the Dover Patrol and was constructed in 1921.

A bracing, undulating circuit – steep in places – along the cliff tops at first, then doubling back through the agricultural hinterland. Some care must be taken on the cliffs, but the views are wonderful. To reach the start of the route, drive north from Dover harbour on the A2. Turn right on to the A258 at the roundabout, then watch for signs for St Margaret's at Cliffe. Drive right through the village and then on down the steep road to the car park by the shore. There is a small fee for parking. PUBLIC TRANSPORT: St Margaret's at Cliffe is on the regular bus route between Folkestone (via Dover) and Deal. Kingsdown is the terminus of a regular bus service from Sandwich (via Deal).

Route description

❶ Walk to the back of the car park and climb up the flight of steps set into the cliffs. Once at the top turn right. Ignore the sign for 'The Leas' to the left and carry straight on.

Walk 24
ST MARGARET'S TO DOVER

7 miles (11 km) there and back   Easy

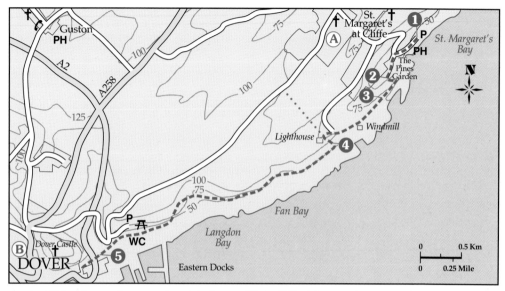

A splendid lineal route along a section of the famous White Cliffs, following clear, rough footpaths and public roads, and providing fine views across the Channel. The route can be started from either end (if started from Dover it can be linked to the St Margaret's to Kingsdown route – Walk 23. To reach St Margaret's, drive north from Dover harbour on the A2. At the first roundabout turn right on to the A258 and watch for the minor road to the right turning down to the village. Drive straight through St Margaret's and then on down the steep road leading to the car park at the foot of the cliffs. There is a small fee for parking. PUBLIC TRANSPORT: St Margaret's is on the regular bus service linking Folkestone (via Dover) and Deal.

Route description

1 Walk back up the road behind the car park and take the first turn to the left (signposted for the Pines Garden). After a short distance turn left onto Beach Road.

2 The road quickly peters out and splits at a multiple junction of tracks. Take the track furthest to the left. This climbs for a short way and then swings to the right. At this point there is a sign for the National Trust property Lighthouse Down.

3 Follow the track past a windmill and on beyond. When it approaches a road cut left, on a rough footpath leading to the entrance of the light-house. Turn left at the gate, following the signpost for the coastal path.

4 Follow the path down to the cliff edge and turn right, noting the views ahead of Dover Castle and harbour. Take particular care while on this section of the route. At various stages alternative paths appear: continue on or near the cliff edge.

5 The path continues until it joins a flight of steps. These drop down under the A2 to join East Cliff on the edge of Dover. Return along one of the alternative paths behind the cliffs.

Points of interest

(A) The village of St Margaret's at Cliffe has one of the finest parish churches in Kent; built in the third quarter of the twelfth century.

(B) Dover, the Gateway to England', has long been the principal port on the south-east coast. The Romans made use of the port, and built a lighthouse on the hill behind (still standing within the precincts of Dover Castle, next to a Saxon church). In later centuries the constable of the castle became *de facto* Warden of the Cinque Ports. Today, Dover is the last of the original Kent Cinque Ports to retain its importance as a harbour, and is the major terminus for cross-Channel ferries. The castle – dating back to the twelfth century, and in continuous military use until after the Second World War – is open to the public.

Walk 25
KEARSNEY

5 miles (8 km)   Moderate

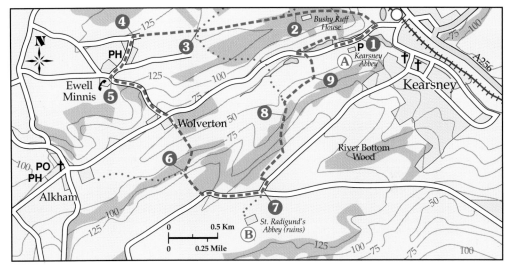

A complicated, undulating circuit through rolling farmland and mixed woodland, following public roads, rough tracks and footpaths. At the end of the walk are the pleasant Russell Gardens. A certain amount of care has to be taken with the route but the countryside is splendid. To reach the start of the route, drive north from the centre of Dover on the A256 road. When it cuts hard right, at a roundabout near the edge of the town, carry straight on. Take the first turn to the left, drive under the railway line, and look for Kearsney Abbey car park to the left. PUBLIC TRANSPORT: Kearsney is a station on the Dover-Canterbury railway line, and is also served by bus services from Dover, Folkestone, Canterbury and Sandwich.

Route description

1 Exit the car park and cross the road. Between Lower Road and the entrance to Kearsney Court there is a broad track. Follow this up the wooded slope to a house.

2 Beyond the house the path becomes fainter. Carry on in the same direction.

3 Go through a gate and continue through a field with the fence to the right. Beyond the next gate the track continues between two fences.

4 When the track reaches a junction turn left down a bridleway, passing the New Castle Inn.

5 At the next junction (telephone box) go hard left and continue down to the main road. Walk across this and follow the bridleway start-

ing opposite. Follow this up to a wood and swing half right.

6 When a track comes in from the right the main track swings left. Follow this down to a quiet road and turn left.

7 At the junction by the entrance to the abbey turn left, then take the first turn to the left, along a broad track. When the main track swings right (into a dump) carry straight on along a smaller footpath.

8 Exit the bottom of the wood and carry straight on towards a gate visible below. Turn right before the gate, through a second gate, and continue across the slope with a fence to the left. At the end of the field cut left, across the fence, then continue with the wood to the right.

9 After a short distance a track opens up to the left, leading down to the road. Turn left along the road for 100 yards until a gap appears in the hedge to the right. Go through this and double back to the right, back to the start.

Points of interest

A Kearsney Abbey was never a real abbey, but simply a large house, completed in 1822, built in the Gothic manner. The café is now housed in the only part of this building to survive.

B St Radigund's was a Premonstratensian abbey, founded in 1192. The buildings fell out of religious use as a result of Henry VIII's dissolution of the monastries in 1538.

Walk 26
FOLKESTONE WARREN

4.5 miles (7 km)   Moderate

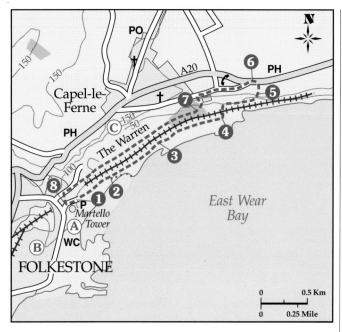

and follow the path along the cliff edge to the Cliff Top Café. Turn left and follow the steps below the café back to the foot of the cliffs.

7 Turn right at the foot of the cliff and follow the track through dense woodland until it joins a tarmac road with a bridge over it. Climb the steps leading up onto the bridge and turn left.

8 Drop down to the tower and turn left along the tarmac road. When the road splits, stay to the left to return to the car park.

Points of interest

A This is one of the string of Martello Towers built along the south coast in the early years of the nineteenth century as part of the defence against a feared attack by Napoleon. They are each three storeys in height and are based upon the plan of the Torre della Mortello in Corsica, which had successfully resisted a British attack in 1794.

B Folkestone originated as a limb of the Cinque Port of Dover, but it did not achieve prominence until, in 1843, the Eastern Railway arrived, linking the town to London. As a result of this link it quickly developed into a thriving seaside resort.

C The Folkestone Warren covers about 350 acres, and represents an area of collapsed chalk cliff. Along this section of the coast, the soft chalk stands on a foundation of harder clay. The combination of wave action from the Channel and subterranean watercourses between the clay and chalk has the effect of undercutting the cliffs, with the result that landslides are not uncommon. These can be quite dramatic: in 1915, thousands of tons of rock came down, burying the railway and altering the line of the cliffs for over 300 yards.

The circuit described here is one of a variety of walks which can be made through this fascinating area of cliffs, shoreline, and densely wooded and fossil-rich undercliff. The climb up the cliffs is quite strenuous, and some care should be taken when walking along the cliff tops. Apart from the natural pleasures of the route – including the tremendous views – there is an example of the numerous Martello Towers which line this part of the coast, near the car park. To reach the start of the route, drive to the eastern end of Folkestone and watch for road signs. PUBLIC TRANSPORT: Folkestone is served by numerous rail and bus services.

Route description

1 Go through the gate at the end of the car park and follow the clear track beyond.

2 At the fork in the track head left, over a small hill (the right-hand track leads down to the shore).

3 The track drops back down towards the shore. Just before reaching it a flight of steps heads off to the left, leading up to rejoin the rail-way line. Continue along the track beside the line.

4 Cross the footbridge over the railway and turn right at the far end. This track leads to a stepped climb to the top of the cliffs.

5 At the top of the cliff cross a stile over a fence and follow the edge of a field to the public road. Turn left.

6 Turn left into Capel-le-Ferne

Walk 27
FOLKESTONE DOWNS

4.5 miles (7 km)   Moderate

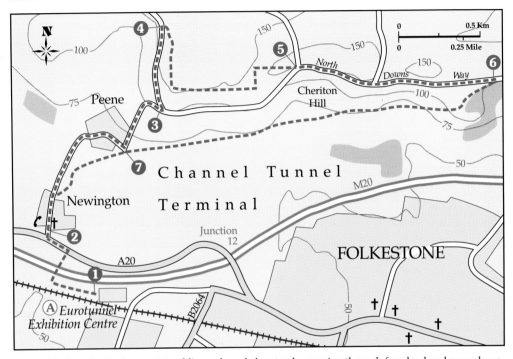

An undulating circuit along quiet public roads and clear tracks, passing through farmland and open downland. The route runs along the ridge of the North Downs, providing wonderful views; not least of the terminal of the Channel Tunnel. Like it or love it, the tunnel represents an extraordinary technical achievement, and this huge site, cradled in a curve of the Downs, provides a novel centrepiece to this route. There is an exhibition centre at the start of the walk. To reach the start of the route, turn off the M20 on the outskirts of Folkestone, following the signs for the exhibition centre. PUBLIC TRANSPORT: Folkestone is on numerous bus and rail services; there is a regular bus service between Folkestone and the Channel Tunnel terminal.

Route description

1 Walk west from the exhibition centre. Turn right over the footbridge over the M20, then cross the A20 (with due care). Turn left, then right to reach the village of Newington.

2 Walk through Newington and then continue along the minor road beyond.

3 After passing through Peene the road reaches a junction. Keep to the left and continue climbing up onto the Downs.

4 Before the road reaches the top of the hill there is a gate to the right with a stile beside it. Cross this and follow the clear track beyond – quickly joining the North Downs Way – along the ridge of the Downs.

5 Cross the small public road and continue beyond.

6 When the path reaches the edge of a wood cut right, down the hill, to the path which runs beside the circuit fence of the Channel Tunnel terminal.

7 When the original road comes in from the right continue along the path, back to Newington.

Points of interest

A The Eurotunnel Exhibition Centre is open daily and explores this amazing transport system. Special features include TV touch-screen displays, scale models of the trains and tunnels, and a viewing tower over the terminal. There is a charge for admittance.

Walk 28
HYTHE

6 miles (9.5 km)   Moderate

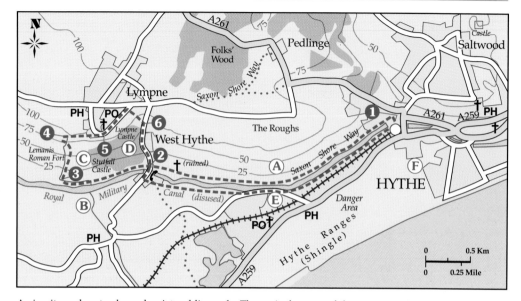

A circuit on clear tracks and quiet public roads. The main features of the route are the nineteenth-century military canal, the Roman remains at Stutfall Castle, Lympne Castle, the miniature railway which follows a part of the route, and the pleasant old town of Hythe. In addition, there are splendid views across Romney Marsh from the path up round Lympne (the path is steep in this section). To reach the start of the route, park somewhere near the canal at the western end of the town. PUBLIC TRANSPORT: There are numerous bus services to Hythe; in addition, the light railway runs along the coast from Dungeness, via New Romney.

Route description

❶ The station for the Romney, Hythe and Dymchurch light railway is at the west end of the town beside the Military Canal. Cross the bridge over the canal by the station and turn left along Green Lane. After a short distance climb up to the left to join the Saxon Shore Way, following the line of the canal.

❷ When the canal is crossed by a public road, cross the road and continue by the side of the canal.

❸ Watch for the Roman ruins on this slope. Slightly beyond them a footbridge crosses the small stream to the right. Cross this and follow

the clear path beyond: turning left after a short way and then jinking right, directly up the slope.

❹ A clear path runs along the top of the slope. Turn right along this, and when the path joins the public road turn right, into the village of Lympne.

❺ Continue past the castle, through the car park, and on along a clear track beyond. At the sign for a public footpath turn right, down the slope.

❻ When the path joins the road turn right, down to the canal (being careful of the traffic on this short stretch). Cross the canal and turn

left onto a clear track leading back to Hythe.

Points of interest

Ⓐ The Saxon Shore Way is the longest of the long-distance footpaths within Kent, running approximately 140 miles from Gravesend, on the Thames Estuary, to the pleasant little town of Rye, just across the border in East Sussex. For most of its length, it follows the present coastline, but in a few places – as here – it cuts inland to remain true to the ancient shoreline. These cliffs would once have looked over the estuary of the Rother and the salt marshes of Romney Marsh beyond.

A diversion to the left at this point leads to the Zoo Park and Gardens at Port Lympne.

(B) The Royal Military Canal was built between 1804-1807 as part of the defences of the south coast against a possible attack by Napoleon (see also Walk 31).

(C) Stutfall Castle is the common name for the few fragments of wall which remain of the Roman fortress of Portus Lemanis, built on a site which then overlooked the sea marshes of Romney Marsh and the northern mouth of the River Rother. The Roman fort was linked to Canterbury by Stone Street (the route of which is now followed by the B2068).

(D) Lympne Castle is thought to be built upon the site of a Roman look-out tower. This may be true, but the oldest sections of the existing structure are Norman, and the greater part of the fabric is fourteenth century. Some later remodelling and building was undertaken by Lorimer in the early twentieth century. The castle was the property of the Archdeacons of Canterbury until 1860. The neighbouring rag-stone church is Norman with thirteenth-century additions.

(E) The light railway was the brain-child of two racing drivers of the 1920s, Captain J.E.P. Howey and Count Zborowski. When the latter was killed in a driving accident Howey continued with the project; laying 14 miles (22.5 km) of 15" gauge track and building locomo-tives and rolling stock to a suitable scale. The line was opened in 1927, and a summer service now operates linking Hythe, Dymchurch, New Romney and Dungeness.

(F) Hythe, at the most easterly point of Romney Marsh, was one of the original Cinque Ports. Initially intended simply as a 'hythe', or quay, for Saltwood, it quickly out-grew its neighbour and became one of the most important of the ports along the south east coast. As with most of the old Kent ports, how-ever, Hythe developed problems with silting in its harbour, and with the eastward drift of the sand and shingle of the coast, which tended to block the harbour entrance. Originally, the harbour was kept relatively clear by the waters of the River Rother, which once reached the sea at this point. However, this particular route of the river (which may have been artificially encour-aged by the Romans) eventually began to dry up, while as early as the reign of Henry III the mouth of the creek was partially blocked by a shingle bar. The advantages of being a Cinque Port, however, were not inconsiderable, and the resi-dents worked hard to retain their privileges – including, amongst other things, freedom from tolls and customs duties. As late as the reign of Elizabeth I, the port was still just about able to fulfil its military oblig-ations (providing eleven ships for the fleet to fight the Spanish Armada), but the crown began to demand ships larger than the silting harbours of Kent could provide, and growing ports such as Portsmouth and Southampton began to outstrip the old Cinque Ports in importance. The last – unsuccessful – attempt to keep Hythe harbour open was made in 1674. The old part of the town, set up on the hillside, is now entirely cut off from the sea.

The current town of Hythe is a pleasant tourist and service centre, forming a small conurbation by linking with the western suburbs of Folkestone. The town is dominated by the cruciform church of St Leonard, which is part Norman and part thirteenth century. The crypt, which dates from the early thir-teenth century, contains some rather grisly relics; a collection of 1100 skulls and a large number of other human bones. These were once thought to be the remains of the dead from some battle, but it now appears that they are a random collection; possibly collected in the crypt when burial space became short during the period of the Black Death in the fourteenth century. Lionel Lukin, the builder of the first lifeboat (in 1785) is buried by the church.

Nearby Saltwood Castle was for a long time the property of the Archbishops of Canterbury. In 1170 (it is reputed) the group of conspira-tors who murdered Thomas á Becket met at the castle before travelling to Canterbury.

Walk 29
WYE

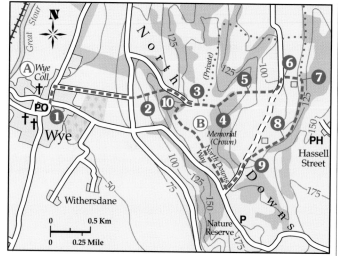

⑥ Turn first right, just before two green water tanks, down a track leading to the left of a farmhouse. Continue beyond on a narrow footpath which joins another concrete track. Turn right along this.

⑦ Follow the track between farm buildings and then through a gate. Ignore the byway cutting off to the left and continue along the track, climbing into a wood. Ignore the bridleway cutting off to the right after a short distance and continue.

⑧ When the path exits the wood carry straight on to a gate. Go through this and continue with trees to the left. At the end of the field pass through another gate, then another a short distance beyond. Once through this, turn right and drop down to join a farm road, to the left of a farm. Turn left.

⑨ When the farm road has almost reached the public road the North Downs Way cuts off to the right. Turn onto this, passing through a gate and continuing with a fence to the right.

⑩ When the path reaches the corner of a field turn right, across a stile, and continue with a wood to the left and a field to the right. Cross two further stiles to rejoin the earlier part of the route. Turn left, then first left down the bridleway, to return to Wye.

Points of interest

Ⓐ Wye College is part of the University of London. The first college on the site was a fifteenth-century priests seminary which was required to close in 1545. Part of the seminary is included in the new college, which was otherwise built in the early twentieth century .

Ⓑ The crown was cut into the hillside in 1901 to commemorate the coronation of Edward VII .

A complicated, undulating circuit (quite steep in places) along quiet public roads, clear tracks, rough footpaths and field boundaries, running through a mixture of farmland, woodland and open downland. The views from the ridge of the North Downs are spectacular. Some care has to be taken with the navigation and there are a number of stiles to be crossed. Dogs should be kept on a lead. Features of the route include the pleasant village of Wye and a crown carved into the chalk of the Downs. To reach the start of the route, drive three miles (5 km) north from the centre of Ashford on the A28 road (for Canterbury), then turn right at the sign for Wye. Park in the centre of the village. PUBLIC TRANSPORT: Wye is served by both trains and buses running between Canterbury and Ashford.

Route description

① Walk along Olantigh Road with the agricultural college to the left. Just before the edge of the village turn right up Occupation Road. A clear track runs up the slope beyond the village, across a metalled road, then on up to the edge of a wood.

② Follow the track through the wood to join another public road. Turn right. Ignore the first footpath cutting off to the right, but when the main track swings to the left carry straight on along a bridleway.

③ When this track swings left (signposted Private) carry straight on once more, towards a wood. Go through a gate in front of the wood and turn left along a clear path.

④ Pass through a gate and continue with a field to the left and the wood to the right. When the trees end cut half right, through the gap, and walk across the field beyond to the gate in the far side.

⑤ Go through the gate and swing left. Upon reaching another fence, turn right down the left-hand edge of the field. At the bottom of the field turn left along a concrete road.

Walk 30
FAGGS WOOD

2 miles (3 km) Easy

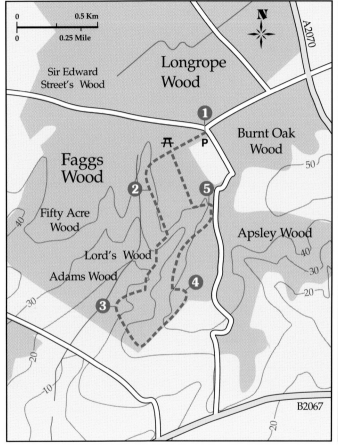

A standard, pleasant forest walk; clear tracks and footpaths, well signposted. To reach the start of the route, drive seven miles (11 km) east of Tenterden on the B2067 (the road for Folkestone). A short distance beyond Warehorne turn left up the minor road signposted for Kingsnorth. After a little over a mile (1.5 km) the road reaches a junction; the car park is to the left at this point. There is no public transport link to the walk.

Route description

❶ Leave the car park along a clear path and follow it: across the end of a clear track and then on to join a second track. Cross this and take the path through the wood beyond, swinging to the left.

❷ Rejoin the main track and continue along it until it reaches a T-junction. Turn right at this point.

❸ Just before the track crosses a small stream a post marks a path cutting off to the left. Follow this up the slope.

❹ When the path rejoins a main track, turn left; then right, soon after, back into the trees.

❺ At the next track, turn left once again; then cut right at the next junction, back to the start.

Walk 31
ROYAL MILITARY CANAL
9 miles (14.5 km)   Difficult

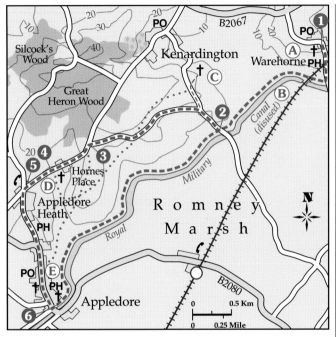

A long circuit: half on quiet public roads (care must be taken on these sections), and half on the paths by the side of a nineteenth-century military canal. The canal runs along the landward edge of Romney Marsh, while the sections along public roads pass through an area of low, rolling farmland. Features of the route include the churches at Warehorne, Kenardington and Appledore, and the small private chapel at Hornes Place. To reach the start of the route, drive six miles (9.5 km) south from Ashford on the A2070. At Hamstreet turn west (right) onto the B2067 and watch for the signs for Warehorne to the left. PUBLIC TRANSPORT: Warehorne, Kenardington and Appledore are all on the route of a bus which runs once daily between Ashford and Lydd.

Route description

1 Walk south from the village along a quiet public road, passing beneath the railway bridge and continuing down to the canal. Turn right along a clear track on the near side of the canal.

2 The canal is crossed by another minor road: turn right along this for a short distance to reach a junction. A short detour to the right – a little over half a mile (1 km) there and back – leads to the church at Kenardington. Otherwise, keep to the left.

3 At the next junction turn to the left (this is a slightly busier road, so be careful).

4 Just beyond the entrance to Gusbourne Farm there is a second turning to the left, leading in to Hornes Place Chapel. Otherwise continue along the road.

5 Swing left into Appledore Heath and follow the road straight through Appledore to return to the canal.

6 Turn left along the near side of the canal to return to the start of the route.

Points of interest

A Warehorne is a small, pleasant assemblage of buildings around a large green. The main body of the church dates from the mid-fourteenth century; the tower from 1776.

B 'With three days east wind', Napoleon observed, 'I could repeat the exploit of William the Conqueror'. From Europe's greatest general, this was not a threat to be taken lightly, and invasion panic quickly gripped the nation. The government's policy for home defence never fully evolved, but some elements were put in place: an attempt was made to remove cattle and foodstuffs from the hinterland of the south-east coast (in the rather pathetic hope of starving the invading army), signal relay stations were set up between the coast and London, and volunteer troops were raised to help with the defence. More constructively, but with no more obvious hope of success, an attempt was made to cut off the vulnerable Romney Marsh coast – an obvious place to land since, as the local smugglers knew, it was very difficult to police adequately – by building a canal along the inland edge of the area.

The canal was started in 1804, and completed in January 1806. The total cost of the project was over £140,000. The resulting waterway was 23 miles long, about nine feet deep and 60 ft wide. It ran from Seabrook, east of Hythe, through Appledore and Rye, to Cliff End, a little beyond Winchelsea. The course of the canal was not straight, but rather a sequence of zig-zags; the point being to make it possible to fire cannon along each section of its length. The north bank of the canal was raised several feet, to provide cover for defenders, and every one and a quarter miles a signal box was erected. Fortunately, the canal was never put to the test: in October 1805, Nelson defeated the French fleet at Trafalgar and effectively removed any realistic threat of invasion. Nevertheless, the canal remained, and during the Second World War it was brought back into service; pillboxes being constructed to replace the cannon of the previous century.

C The original sections of the church at Kenardington were built in the thirteenth century, though there have been later additions. The peculiar truncated shape of the church is due to lightning: the building was struck in 1559, after which the nave and chancel were demolished.

D Hornes Place Chapel is a small private chapel, built in the fourteenth century (it and the attached house were attacked by Wat Tyler in 1381). It is open to the public on Wednesdays.

E Appledore was once an important port at the head of the estuary of the River Rother. There was a Saxon fort on the site, which was attacked and taken by the invading Danes in the great raid of 892. 250 ships were brought up the River Rother from Hythe and drawn up by the river while the invaders plundered the surrounding area and then negotiated their terms of withdrawal with King Alfred. In the late thirteenth century a storm changed the course of the Rother and left the town high and dry. The church was rebuilt after 1380 (when it was destroyed in a French raid), and received further additions in the sixteenth century.

Walk 32
STONE IN OXNEY

5 miles (8 km)   Easy

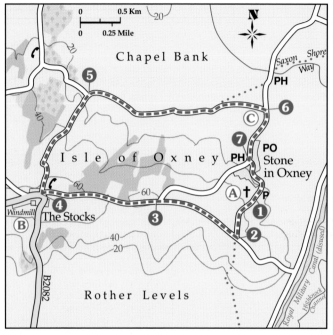

④ A four-way junction. Turn right (signposted for 'Ebony').
⑤ Turn right at the junction (signposted for 'Appledore').
⑥ Turn right at the junction (signposted for 'Stone').
⑦ Turn left at the sign for 'Stone Church'. Crown Inn on the corner.

Points of interest

Ⓐ St Mary's Church dates from 1464 (when it was rebuilt after a fire), and was renovated in the nineteenth century. It seems, however, to stand on a far older religious site: within the church stands a block of ragstone, unearthed from beneath the chancel two centuries ago, with the outline of an ox on either side and marks of fire on the top. This is thought to be a Roman shrine to Mithras, and may have some connection with the name 'Stone in Oxney' ('Oxney' means 'oxen island'). Beside the church there is a fine fifteenth-century house. Oxney remained a true island until Walland Marsh became fully walled in 1562.

Ⓑ The windmill at Stocks dates from the late eighteenth century.

Ⓒ At this point it is possible to make a link with Walk 31, by the Royal Military Canal. Instead of turning right at this junction, turn left. Follow the road down to the inn by the sewer; cross the bridge and turn right onto the Saxon Shore Way footpath. It is a little under two miles (3 km) from this junction to Appledore, where the canal can be joined.

An undulating circuit entirely on quiet public roads (be careful while walking along these roads). Stone in Oxney is on the eastern end of Isle of Oxney: at one time an island on the edge of the broad sea marshes of Walland Marsh, but now an area of quiet farmland and woodland. This route provides views across the agricultural levels to north, east and south which were once muddy, tidal channels. It also passes the interesting old church at Stone in Oxney. To reach the start of the route, drive north from Rye on the A268. Just beyond the edge of the town turn onto the B2082 and follow it for four miles (6.5 km) to The Stocks. Turn east at this point onto the minor road to Stone in Oxney and park in the small National Trust car park opposite the church. PUBLIC TRANSPORT: A very occasional bus service between Tenterden and Rye (running only on Thursdays and Fridays) stops at the village.

Route description

① Start from the car park opposite the church and walk south along the quiet public road (ie, uphill).

② Turn right at the junction (signposted for 'Wittersham').

③ Turn left at the junction (signposted for 'Wittersham').

Walk 33
WITTERSHAM

5 miles (8 km)   Moderate

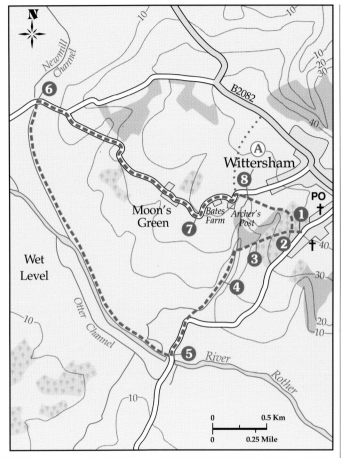

A quite complicated circuit through mixed farmland; passing through fields, along clear tracks and quiet public roads, and by the banks of the River Rother. Some care should be taken on the public road sections. Wittersham is on the western end of Isle of Oxney, and five centuries ago this route would have followed the winding stream in the middle of a muddy, tidal creek; now it passes through a fertile and prosperous farming region. To reach the start of the route, drive north from Rye on the A268 road for Tonbridge. One mile (1.5 km) out of the town, turn right onto the B2082. Wittersham is about four miles (6.5 km) along this road. PUBLIC TRANSPORT: Wittersham is on a regular bus route between Tenterden and Rye.

Route description

1 Starting from the lynch gate of the church, cross the road and walk down the public footpath which starts directly opposite.

2 After a short distance cut left, across a stile, then walk diagonally across the orchard beyond.

3 Cross a double stile at the far corner of the orchard and then go directly across the field beyond. Cross a further stile, and a footbridge beyond, then turn left across a stile and continue with a fence to the right and a stream to the left.

4 Cross a further stile and continue by the stream, then continue down the left-hand sides of two fields (crossing stiles where required) before climbing up to join a small public road to the left. Turn right along this.

5 When the road reaches the River Rother turn right (on its near side), through two gates and then on along the river bank.

6 Climb onto the road which crosses the river and turn right. Turn right again at the first junction (signposted for Moon's Green).

7 The road swings round to the left, passing Bates Farm and Archer's Post. Immediately after the latter a public footpath starts to the right. Turn down this.

8 Cross a stile and continue down a narrow field with a fence to the right, then cross a further stile to enter a band of woodland. Follow the clear footpath beyond back to the church .

Points of interest

A Wittersham is the main settlement on Isle of Oxney. Its church is largely 14th century, based on an existing 13th-century building. The tower dates from the 16th century. Opposite the church is Wittersham House, designed by Lutyens in the early twentieth century.

Walk 34
OLD ROMNEY TO NEW ROMNEY   3 miles (5 km) one way   Moderate

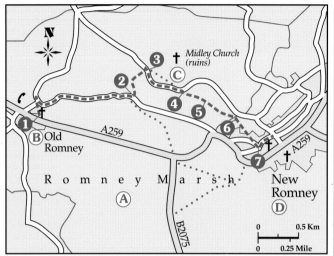

Midley Church
(ruins)

A short, lineal route between two of the towns of Romney Marsh. There are no paths, and a certain amount of navigation is required when crossing the various fields, but the terrain is flat and the church tower ahead is a useful guide. This walk links two of the famous churches of the area, and gives a good example of the bleak charm of this peculiar district. To reach the start of the route (which can be linked with Walk 35), drive ten miles (16 km) east of Rye on the A259 (the road for Old Romney to New Romney). There is a small car park at the church. PUBLIC TRANSPORT: There is a regular bus link between the two villages, and New Romney can be reached by a variety of bus services, in addition to lying on the light railway line between Hythe and Dungeness.

Route description
❶ Starting from the church at Old Romney, walk back along Church Close towards the public road. Before reaching it double back along a clear track flanked by houses. After a little under a mile there is a sign to the left for a footpath.
❷ Turn into an arable field and walk across: parallel to the power lines at first, then swinging towards the right-hand end of a group of trees, visible ahead, which marks the point where a farm track joins the public road.

❸ Turn right along the road for about half a mile (1 km), until it swings hard left, then (just beyond the entrance to a farm road) cross a stile to the right of the road.
❹ Having crossed the stile, continue in the original direction. Walk parallel to the fence, which is to the left, until it curves away towards the road. Continue as before, keeping an eye open ahead for the tower of New Romney Church. When this becomes visible (it is hidden by trees at first) head slightly to the left of it.

❺ A stile becomes visible in the fence ahead. Head for this, then aim straight for the church tower beyond. After a short distance a prominent white gable appears ahead: head towards this, crossing a small stream on a footbridge.
❻ Beyond the bridge follow the line of the left-hand fence through four small fields, crossing stiles between each. The last stile leads on to a public road (Spitalfield Lane) with houses on either side. Turn left.
❼ At the end of the lane turn left into Sussex Road and follow it to its junction with Ashford Road. Turn right for the centre of the town; left to reach the start of the route to St Mary in the Marsh (Walk 35).

Points of interest
Ⓐ Romney Marsh is one of those odd corners of the country which have so distinctive a character that they seem to generate a mystique of their own. On the face of it, there is little to recommend the place: flat, with few towns or buildings, and riddled with a multitude of apparently randomly twisting drainage channels. Nevertheless, it has always found its admirers. One such – the novelist Ford Madox Ford, who lived around its fringes for some years – wrote of the misleading impression of its own vastness which it gave the pedestrian, and of the silence which 'is the characteristic of the place, a brooding silence, an inconceivably self-centred abstraction. . . One counts for so little'. Another – Richard Barnham, rector of Snargate church and author of The Ingoldsby Legends – wrote that 'the world is divided into five parts, namely Europe, Asia, Africa, America and Romney Marsh'. For some reason, it has always been able to sink its hooks in a certain type of person.

The name Romney Marsh is often used loosely to refer to the entire low-lying peninsula in the triangle formed by Rye, Hythe and Dungeness. Technically, however, the name refers only to that section of the marsh which lies to the east of the Rhee Wall – the line of which is now followed by the road linking Appledore and New Romney. Work appears to have been started in this area by the Romans; gradually walling and draining the higher sections of ground. Whether or not they built the Rhee Wall itself – not so much a wall, in fact, as an artificial channel, flanked by raised banks, restraining and directing the River Rother on its route to the sea – is uncertain; it may have been built by the Saxons, and is first mentioned in a document as late as 1258. Whoever was responsible, however, it appears to have helped to accelerate the process of reclamation; individual landowners each enclosing and draining the sections of marsh adjacent to their own holdings (hence the haphazard nature of the region's drainage channels). Work was begun on the neighbouring Walland and Denge Marshes in the eleventh and twelfth centuries, but they were not finally walled until the sixteenth century.

The reason for all this effort and expense was that the land, once reclaimed, was extremely fertile – a fact which attracted the wealthiest landowners; notably the church. Some lands in the Marsh had belonged to various abbeys and churches from Saxon times – King Offa granted land in the area to Christchurch, Canterbury, in AD774 – and by the middle of the thirteenth century, virtually the entire area was in the hands of various religious houses.

In the later Middle Ages, Dutch engineers were brought to the Marsh to attempt to strengthen its sea defences, and in the early sixteenth century a serious effort was made to construct a lasting sea wall (the current, concrete wall was built following the bad flooding of 1953). The area thus enclosed proved to be particularly suitable for the rearing of sheep, and, wool being England's most valuable export at the time, the Marsh soon became both populous and prosperous. This fact can be observed in the number of large churches in the area which were clearly built for a larger congregation than could possibly be assembled now. Fairfield stands quite on its own; Old Romney, Ivychurch, Snargate, St Mary in the Marsh, Burmarsh and others in tiny villages or hamlets: a memorial to the region's past wealth. These churches provide a great part of the charm of the place. Generally Norman in origin, the vicissitudes of history have led them to be rebuilt, remodelled or added to over the centuries, with the result that they now represent an odd amalgamation of the canons of ecclesiastical architecture with less bookish vernacular invention. They are buildings, above all, of great character.

In addition to sheep-rearing, the marshes developed a considerable reputation for smuggling; the long, low coast and mass of internal waterways making the area notoriously difficult to police. Most villages have stories of their association with the illicit trade, and their churches seem often to have been used as depots for the smuggled tobacco and spirits. Nowadays, the interior of the Marsh is a much quieter place: an area of wide fields, isolated farmhouses and small villages linked by twisting roads and the maze of drainage ditches. The sea coast is more populous, with a row of quiet resorts behind the protection of the sea wall.

Ⓑ Old Romney, a tiny village straddling the line of the old Rhee Wall, originally occupied a low island in the marshes. It had access to the sea, and the Domesday survey noted the existence of local fisheries. There was also, at one time, a manor house, the moat of which is still visible to the north of the village. The church appears to be thirteenth century with later additions.

Ⓒ The ruin to the left at this point is all that remains of Midley Church.

Ⓓ New Romney was 'new' in Saxon times; being mentioned as early as AD740, when it was described as a fishing hamlet. It appears to have been built as a planned town: its long, narrow shape reflecting the contours of the low island which it occupied at the mouth of the Rother Estuary. The town became one of the original Cinque Ports, and a settlement of some importance (with a population of 5000 in 1380). At that time, the church – a large Norman structure, with fourteenth century additions – stood behind the town wharf, and ships were able to tie up to its walls. In 1287, however, a great storm broke through the marsh defences, flooding the town (the flood marks are still visible on the columns inside the church) and changing the course of the River Rother so that it reached the sea at Rye instead of Romney. A second storm, in 1334, completed the destruction of New Romney harbour, and the attempt to maintain the navigable link with Appledore was abandoned. Until the nineteenth century, however, a large bay, Romney Hoy, remained to the east of the town: the remnant of the old estuary.

Deprived of its harbour, New Romney now depends for its prosperity on its role as a service centre for the surrounding agricultural land.

Walk 35

NEW ROMNEY TO ST MARY IN THE MARSH 3 miles (5 km) one way Moderate

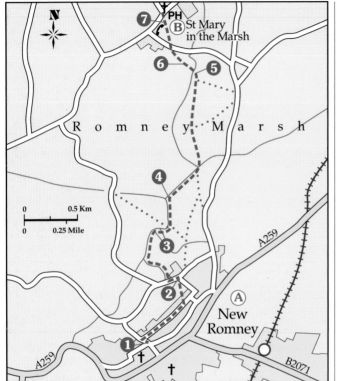

❷ On the far side of the field is a tarmac road. Turn left along this until the field to the right ends. At this point there is a sign for the public footpath. Turn right into the field and walk along with a small channel down to the left.

❸ The channel swings round until it is pointing back towards New Romney, at which point there is a footbridge to the left. Cross this and continue with the channel to the left. At the end of the field a larger sewer crosses the way: turn right beside this.

❹ Follow this sewer for about 400 yards until it is crossed by a footbridge. Cross this, then continue with a channel to the left. When this swings away to the left, carry straight on (aiming for the right-hand end of the houses visible to the right of the church).

❺ When the channel swings back in from the left, look for a footbridge over it. Cross this and climb the bank on the far side. Follow a path across the field beyond, heading for the right-hand end of a large shed, visible ahead.

❻ The path leads to a stile. Cross the field beyond this, heading towards a further stile to the right of the shed. Walk straight across the road beyond to a further stile, then head directly towards the church.

❼ At the corner of the field there is a small gate. Go through this and turn right (with the Star Inn to the right) to cross the bridge in the centre of the village. The church is directly ahead.

Points of interest

Ⓐ New Romney (see Walk 34).
Ⓑ St Mary in the Marsh is a small group of buildings with an inn and a fine church. The latter is largely late thirteenth century, but with a Norman tower.

A short, lineal route (a possible extension of Walk 34) between two of the villages of Romney Marsh. There are some footpaths running by the various dykes and sewers, but a certain amount of navigation may be required when the route sets off over fields (walkers are requested to take all due care when crossing fields, and to avoid damaging crops). The flat countryside and the tower of the church of St Mary in the Marsh can help with navigation. To reach the start of the route, park in the centre of New Romney and look for the bottom of Ashford Road. PUBLIC TRANSPORT: There are numerous bus services to New Romney, which is also on the line of the light railway running between Hythe and Dungeness.

Route description

❶ From the centre of New Romney, turn north-west onto Ashford Road (the minor road to Ivychurch), then turn right from this on to Rolfe Lane. A public footpath is signposted between numbers 67 and 69. Cross a stile at the end of the gardens and walk straight across the field beyond.